Islamic State

Islamic State

Rewriting History

Michael Griffin

PlutoPress

www.plutobooks.com

First published 2016 by Pluto Press
345 Archway Road, London N6 5AA

www.plutobooks.com

British Library Cataloguing in Publication Data
A catalogue record for this book is available from the British Library

ISBN   978 0 7453 3656 5   Hardback
ISBN   978 0 7453 3651 0   Paperback
ISBN   978 1 7837 1711 8   PDF eBook
ISBN   978 1 7837 1713 2   Kindle eBook
ISBN   978 1 7837 1712 5   EPUB eBook

This book is printed on paper suitable for recycling and made from
fully managed and sustained forest sources. Logging, pulping and
manufacturing processes are expected to conform to the environmental
standards of the country of origin.

Typeset by Stanford DTP Services, Northampton, England
Text design by Melanie Patrick
Simultaneously printed by CPI Antony Rowe, Chippenham, UK
and Edwards Bros in the United States of America

Contents

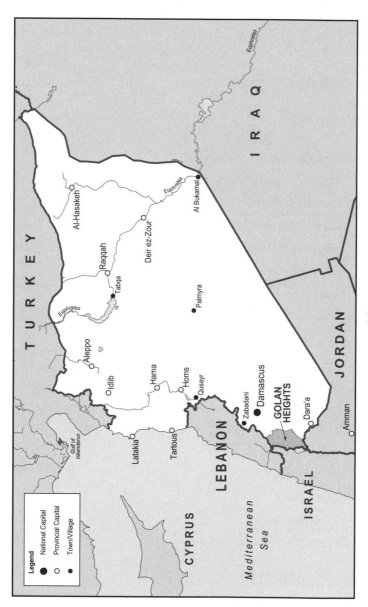

Map 1

Map 2

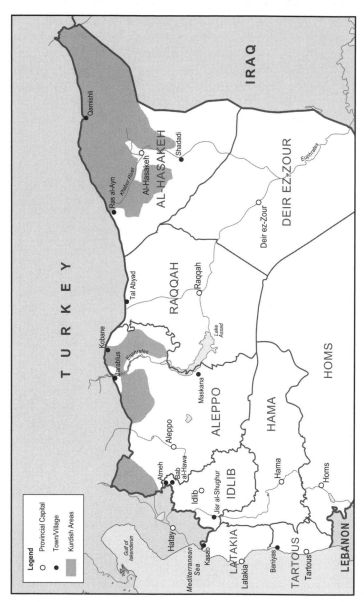

Map 3

List of Acronyms/Abbreviations

AQI	Al Qaeda in Iraq
CERS	Scientific Studies and Research Centre
FSA	Free Syrian Army
IEDs	Improvised Explosive Devices
IAI	Islamic Army in Iraq
INM	Iraqi National Movement
IS	Islamic State
ISF	Iraqi Security Forces
ISI	Islamic State of Iraq
ISIS	Islamic State of Iraq and al-Sham
JaN	Jabhat al-Nusra
JASW	Jaysh Ahl al-Sinnah wal Jama'a
JRTN	Jaysh Rijal al-Tariq al-Naqshbandi
LCCs	Local Coordination Committees
MA	Mujahideen Army
MCTRF	Military Council of Tribal Revolutionaries of Fallujah
MIT	Millî İstihbarat Teşkilatı (Turkish intelligence)
MNF–I	Multi-National Force – Iraq
MSC	Mujahideen Shura Council
NTC	National Transitional Council
SMC	Supreme Joint Military Command
SNC	Syrian National Council
SOFA	Status of Forces Agreement

Timeline

2000

Musab al-Zarqawi establishes a training camp in Afghanistan and forms Al-Tawhid wal-Jihad (Monotheism and Holy War).

2002

March   Al-Zarqawi relocates to Kurdish Iraq.

2004

October   After declaring allegiance to Osama bin Laden, al-Zarqawi changes his group's name to Al Qaeda in Iraq (AQI).

2005

November   AQI merges with five other groups to form Mujahideen Shura Council.

2006

7 June   Al-Zarqawi killed in US airstrike.

17 September   Tribes in Anbar hold a Day of Awakening to denounce AQI.

15 October   AQI alters name to Islamic State of Iraq (ISI), with Abu Omar al-Baghdadi as caliph or supreme leader.

30 December   Execution of Saddam Hussein.

2007

January   Additional 20,000 US troops arrive in Iraq to implement the 'Surge'.

15 June   Operation Phantom Thunder is launched to clear Baghdad of ISI and Shia militias.

2010

18 April	Abu Omar al-Baghdadi and Abu Ayyub al-Masri, ISI war minister, are killed in an airstrike.
18 December	Start of Tunisia's Jasmine Revolution.

2011

11 February	President Mubarak of Egypt resigns after millions demonstrate.
15 February	Protests against President Ghaddafi lead to civil war.
15 March	Arrest and torture of a dozen teenagers for spraying graffiti in Dara'a sparks nationwide protests.
19 March	NATO, supported by Qatar and United Arab Emirates, launches airstrikes on Ghaddafi's defences and imposes a no-fly zone over Libya.
15 April	Syrian security forces besiege Dara'a.
2 May	Killing of Osama bin Laden.
18 May	United States imposes sanctions on Syrian officials for human rights abuses.
4 June	72 killed in Hama as 50,000 gather at 'Friday of Children' protest.
1 July	Hundreds of thousands of Syrians participate in protests across the country.
29 July	Defecting officers announce creation of Free Syrian Army (FSA).
5 August	Regime kills hundreds of civilians in Hama.
23 August	Exiled opposition leaders forms Syrian National Council (SNC) in Istanbul.
4 October	Russia and China veto UN resolution imposing sanctions on Syria.

21 October	President Obama announces withdrawal of last US troops from Iraq.
8 November	UN estimates Syrian death toll at 3,500.
12 November	Arab League suspends Syria's membership, imposes sanctions.
11 December	United States completes Iraqi withdrawal.
15 December	Iraqi Prime Minister Nouri al-Maliki charges Sunni Vice-President Tariq al-Hashemi with supporting terrorism.
23 December	Two suicide car bombs kill 44 in the first major attacks in Damascus.
28 December	Security forces open fire on 20,000 protesters in Hama the day before Arab League visit.

2012

6 January	Suicide bomber kills 26 in Damascus' Al-Midan neighbourhood. Jabhat al-Nusra (JaN) claims responsibility.
23 January	JaN releases first video.
4 February	Russia and China veto UN resolution backing Arab League plan calling for Bashar al-Assad to step down.
8 February	Al Qaeda's Ayman al-Zawahiri urges Muslims to support Syrian uprising.
22 February	Reporter Marie Colvin and photographer Remi Ochlik killed by regime fire in Baba Amr district of Homs.
6 March	SNC is given Syria's seat in the Arab League.
April	SNC announces it will pay salaries to officers and soldiers of the FSA.
1 May	UN-brokered ceasefire collapses after violations by regime and opposition.

27 May	Pro-Assad forces kill 108 civilians, including 48 children, in Sunni town of Taldou, Houla region.
4 June	ISI kills 26, wounds 190 in suicide attack on Shia Endowment in Bab al-Muadham, Baghdad.
6 June	Assad appoints new prime minister, Riyad Hijab, after winning 90 per cent in elections.
16 June	United States closes embassy in Syria.
30 June	Geneva Action Group on Syria (Geneva I) agrees on the need 'for a transitional government body with full executive powers'. Neither government nor opposition attend.
18 July	Bomb at National Security Building in Damascus kills ministers of defence and interior, and Assad's brother-in-law, Assef Shawkhat.
19 July	Kurdish People's Protection Units occupy Kobane and other Kurdish-majority towns.
July	Regime launches aerial attacks in rebel-held towns and villages in Aleppo, Idlib and Latakia provinces, hitting hospitals and bread queues.
21 July	Abu Bakr al-Baghdadi opens 'Destroying the Walls' campaign.
23 July	Syria threatens to use chemical weapons if subjected to foreign attack.
23 July	ISI detonates 30 truck and car bombs at different locations in Iraq in one day.
6 August	Riyad Hijab defects to Jordan after serving only two months as Syria's prime minister.

2 August	Calling the task 'mission impossible', Kofi Annan resigns as UN-Arab League peace envoy to Syria. UN announces casualties have surpassed 20,000 deaths.
20 August	President Obama says the United States will reconsider opposition to military intervention if Syria crosses a 'red line' by using chemical weapons.
August	First reported use of 'barrel bombs' by regime on civilian areas.
27 September	Attack on Tikrit's Tasfirat prison secures release of 100 militants, 47 of whom are on death row.
9 October	Syrian air force fires cluster bombs at opposition in Idlib, Homs, Aleppo, Latakia and Damascus suburb of Eastern Ghouta.
28 November	JaN claims responsibility for 40 of the 49 suicide bombings recorded since December 2011.
11 December	Obama recognises Syrian National Opposition Coalition as official opposition; designates JaN a terrorist organisation linked to Al Qaeda.
21 December	Sunnis stage mass rallies after Prime Minister al-Maliki orders arrest of Finance Minister Rafi al-Issawi's bodyguards.

2013

16 January	Regime aircraft kill 80 civilians at Aleppo University on first day of exams.
12 February	UN High Commissioner for Human Rights blames UN Security Council for lack of progress on civil war, as death toll passes 60,000.

25 February	*New York Times* reports large-scale shipments of Croatian weapons to Syrian rebels by Saudi Arabia.
4 March	JaN, Ahrar al-Sham and other rebel groups capture Raqqah, the first provincial capital to fall since the start of the uprising.
6 March	ISIS leads capture of Aleppo's Menagh airbase after 10-month siege.
Mid-April	Hezbollah leads regime offensive at al-Qusayr, staging point for rebel arms shipments from Lebanon.
9 April	Abu Bakr al-Baghdadi announces a name change from ISI to the Islamic State in Iraq and al-Sham (ISIS), and claims JaN is a subordinate ISIS command.
10 April	JaN leader Abu Mohammed al-Julani rejects merger with ISIS, declares allegiance to Al Qaeda.
23 April	Iraqi forces kill 50 Sunni demonstrators at anti-government sit-in in Hawija, prompting clashes in Mosul and Fallujah.
25 April	US intelligence accuses Assad of using chemical weapons, but says the data is not solid enough to warrant intervention.
13 May	Syrian Observatory of Human Rights estimates death toll at 94,000–120,000, of whom 41,000 are Alawites.
May	Iraqi forces launch counter-attack in western Anbar and northern Diyala provinces.
27 May	EU ends embargo on sending weapons to Syrian rebels.

4 June	Al-Zawahiri orders ISIS and JaN to retain separate commands in Iraq and Syria, and encourages mediation.
13 June	President Obama authorises lethal aid to Syrian rebels after the United States finds conclusive evidence of use of chemical weapons.
14 June	Abu Bakr al-Baghdadi rejects Al Qaeda's guidance, and vows to build an Islamic state in two countries.
July	ISIS attack on Abu Ghraib prison kills 68 security forces and releases 500 fighters.
29 July	Abu Bakr al-Baghdadi announces 'Soldiers' Harvest' campaign.
21 August	Chemical weapons attacks in Damascus kill 1,400 civilians.
21 August	Regime launches Operation Capital Shield in Damascus.
30 August	House of Commons rejects by 285 to 272 a government motion to intervene in Syria.
31 August	President Obama says he will seek Congressional authorisation for use of military force against Syria.
9 September	Russia proposes Syria surrenders its chemical arsenal.
11 September	President Obama asks Congress to postpone vote authorising military action in Syria.
23 September	ISIS clashes with FSA-linked forces in northern Aleppo, takes control of Bab al-Hawa border crossing.
22 November	Seven rebel groups create Islamic Front, with Saudi Arabian support.

9 December	Syria Martyrs Brigade, along with 13 other FSA groups, forms Syria Revolutionaries Front in response to the creation of the Islamic Front.
11 December	Islamic Front captures Bab al-Hawa border crossing and Babisqa warehouses.
18 December	JaN leader, Abu Mohammed al-Julani gives his first interview to Al Jazeera.

2014

3 January	ISIS takes control of Fallujah and parts of Ramadi.
January	Fighting breaks out between Islamic Front and ISIS after killing of Ahrar al-Sham's commander, Abu Rayyan.
7 January	White House announces it will supply Iraq with drones and Hellfire missiles.
22 January–15 February	Geneva II hosts first direct talks between Syria's Deputy Foreign Minister Faisal al-Moqdad and Ahmad al-Jarba, head of the SNC, without substantive progress. Islamic Front rejects Geneva process.
3 February	Al-Zawahiri formally severs all ties between Al Qaeda and ISIS.
22 February	UN Security Council Resolution demands all parties in Syria cease the use of barrel bombs in populated areas.
24 February	Al Qaeda negotiator Abu Khalid al-Suri is killed by ISIS suicide bomber.
14 March	Activists estimate 5,000–6,000 barrel bombs have been dropped in populated areas since August 2012, killing 20,000 people, with 556 on Aleppo between 25 December and 10 February.

30 March	ISIS launches offensive into JaN-held areas of Deir ez-Zour province.
30 April	Iraqis vote in parliamentary elections.
June	Pro-Assad Iraqi Shia fighters withdraw to Iraq to aid in fighting ISIS.
10 June	ISIS captures Mosul.
11 June	ISIS captures Tikrit.
15 June	ISIS captures Tal Afar.
19 June	United States announces deployment of 300 military advisors to re-train Iraqi army.
23 June	UN declares all Syrian chemical weapons have been removed.
29 June	ISIS announces new caliphate and changes name to 'Islamic State'.
4 July	Delta Force commandoes fail to find US hostages, James Foley and Stephen Sotloff, in secret operation near Raqqah.
14 July	JaN withdraws from Deir ez-Zour, ceding control to IS.
25 July	IS captures Syrian Army base in Raqqah and beheads many soldiers.
2–3 August	IS defeats *peshmerga* at Sinjar and Zumar, as thousands of Yazidis seek refuge.
3 August	IS captures Mosul Dam.
8 August	President Obama authorises airstrikes in Iraq to protect Yazidi refugees and defend the Iraqi Kurdish capital of Irbil.
12 August	United States announces it will send 130 advisors to Iraq.
15 August	Prime Minister al-Maliki agrees not to seek a third term and is replaced by Haider al-Abadi, deputy speaker in parliament.

19 August	James Foley is executed.
24 August	Al-Taqba Airbase falls to IS.
17 September	US Senate votes a $500 million arms and training programme to boost moderate Syrian groups opposed to both Assad and IS.
19–22 September	200,000 refugees leave Kobane as IS advances into the area.
22–27 September	Aircraft from the United States, Saudi Arabia, Jordan and the United Arab Emirates target JaN positions in Aleppo and Idlib, and IS command and manpower, oil production facilities and heavy armour in Raqqah and Deir ez-Zour governorates.
14 October	US airdrops arms, ammunition, food and medical supplies to Kurdish forces defending Kobane.
20 October	Turkey allows *peshmerga* to transit through its borders to reinforce Kurdish forces in Kobane. Siege continues until 26 January 2015.
2 December	Syrian Observatory of Human Rights reports total losses since March 2011 of 300,000, of whom 63,070 were civilians, 44,237 security forces, 34,383 rebels and Islamists, 22,624 foreign fighters and 28,974 pro-regime militia members. UN estimates 220,000 killed by 15 January 2015.

Preface

Heroes are in tombs, real men are in prison, and traitors are in palaces.

Seifeddine Razgui[1]

It seemed a good idea to track the development of the Islamic State (IS) from its origins in the US occupation of Iraq to the present, before it disappeared behind the smokescreen of its own vicious celebrity, leaving footnotes, like breadcrumbs, for those following other lines of enquiry in the labyrinth of disinformation and corrupted faith within which it operates.

Thus, in theory, a contour map might emerge of a movement that seems perfectly and hermetically sealed against the invasive curiosity of outsiders, tending to preserve the quintessential secrecy required of a group that derives a vast amount of its awe from the ability to inspire defeatism among its foes through gestures of raw cruelty and religious braggadocio.

There were points of comparison between IS and the rise of the Taliban movement in Afghanistan 20 years earlier, and at first glimpse IS seemed just as shrouded in calculated obscurity and religious obscurantism as the Pashtun militia had once been. Saudi Arabia and Pakistan's empowerment of the Taliban – and Al Qaeda – found echoes in the struggles of Saudi Arabia, Qatar and Turkey to harness the Syrian revolution to their own designs, a rivalry that might credibly have spawned a proxy force, like the IS, to devour popular resistance to the regime of Bashar al-Assad, and dissipate its democratic aspirations in the futile pursuit of a totalitarian Islamic state.

But there the similarities end. Still newcomers to the play-book of international jihad, Qatar and Turkey had neither the will nor the funds to sustain the monster IS ultimately became, even by misadventure, while Saudi Arabia, with the benefits of hindsight after 9/11, had effectively ring-fenced donations by its more reckless donors to minimise just the type of blowback that now threatens the kingdom.

IS, moreover, eclipsed Al Qaeda as a threat to the West by re-casting its focus on the Shia and other non-Sunni communities, and sublimating the energies of the international recruitment pool towards building a visionary caliphate – rather than the overthrow of any state. More intriguingly, IS has never seriously menaced Israel, apart from beheading Steven Sotloff, a freelance journalist with Israeli citizenship, indicating a tacit understanding between the Islamic state and the Zionist state not to meddle in one another's affairs.

This, and the broader complexity of a proxy war in Syria between Iran and Saudi Arabia, and their respective allies, lay beyond the remit of this book, which confines itself to a chronological approach to IS in the Middle East, and not its subsequent expansion from Afghanistan to Nigeria.

The speed with which the defeated forerunner of the IS recovered after US forces withdrew from Iraq in late 2011 hinted at supplies of secret money, either from radical Gulf billionaires or Saddam Hussein's legendary nest-egg – allegedly, proceeds from the UN Oil-for-Food Programme sequestered in Syria's banking system against just such a rainy day. But to insist on either as supporting the running costs of an organisation that, by some estimates, fields up to 100,000 personnel – from civilian administrators, police, engineers, teachers, mechanics, recruiters, guards and, least numerous of all, combat fighters, including their dependants and widows – is to succumb to a myth as transparent as the argument that

IS funded itself by robbing the Mosul banks of $450 million, protection rackets, sales of the crudest of crude oil or the auction of Assyrian antiquities to Western collectors.

It doesn't add up: no convincing, open-source material is available to explain how IS operates financially day to day, and there is remarkably little interest in securing more precise data on the question.

IS resists analysis as fiercely as it repels any other form of penetration, while the context in which it thrives grows more complex by the week, suggesting that we are witnessing a phenomenon that obeys none of the narrative rules previously encountered. Everything that can be known about it is either inferred, informed by hyperbolic speculation or simply placed into the public domain by the caliph, Abu Bakr al-Baghdadi, and his advisors, based on IS' own understanding of what the market – the mission, the recruitment base, the fear metric – can tolerate, as well as an astute reading of the attention span of its audiences from Baghdad to the Washington Beltway.

Any history of the rise of IS, perforce, constitutes an account of the many US failures to develop a consistent policy focus in the Middle East after the withdrawal of forces from Iraq at the end of 2011, a period that spans the optimism of the Arab Spring revolutions, among which just one – Tunisia – now survives on life-support. The most clinical example where more aggressive US intervention might have curtailed the killing of Syrian civilians and also nipped IS in the bud was its failure to punish the Assad regime for using sarin gas in rebel-held districts of Damascus and smaller cities in 2013.

There were other tipping points, but that particular loss of nerve signalled most forcefully to the Syrian regime and its sponsors, Iran and Russia, that the United States would wink at any atrocity to avoid involvement. That scenario is relatively unaltered two years later as a policy of limited airstrikes, limited training for Iraqi forces and limited arms for Syrian rebels are expected to yield limited results by the time the Obama presidency ends in 2016.

One theme that runs through IS like a golden thread is jail-time. As well as formidable organisational gifts, Abu Musab al-Zarqawi's most memorable bequest was an extreme form of spiritual discipline, forged in one of the world's harshest prisons, which colonised the US army's largest holding facility for Iraqi terrorism suspects at Camp Bucca, and fanned out to infect thousands of potential Sunni militants when the primary carriers were released.

How this strain of intense sectarianism fused with the more secular tendencies of veteran Baathists in Iraq – even as Syria's Baathists remained immune – is a mystery, yet it produced a cadre of self-sufficient and ruthless fighters, who drank from the same spring of martyrdom and prophecy.

Very like Spartacus, but more so.

1

The Great Escape

Camp Bucca was still being built in the desert as the pictures from Abu Ghraib tumbled out: the pyramid of naked men; a prisoner forced to masturbate in front of a female American jailer; the hooded scarecrow, wires attached for mock, electro-shock torture, in a stance not unlike crucifixion.

These primitive selfies of routine abuse redefined the US-led invasion of Iraq in March 2003, swelling the mounting grievances of its large Sunni minority. Stripped of power after the overthrow of Saddam Hussein, himself a Sunni, they were denied any role in the new Iraq after being summarily dismissed from their jobs in the armed forces, intelligence agencies and broad sectors of the civilian administration. As many as half a million Sunnis, many trained for combat, were suddenly out of work and poor.

Camp Bucca was intended as a model detention facility along American lines, equally mindful of the needs of its prisoners and the future of penal detention in Iraq. 'We want the prisoners to say, "The Americans treated me alright and they're good-hearted people", Col. Jim Brown told US journalists on a tour in mid-January 2005.[1]

Sprawling across two square miles of sand and rock near the port of Umm Qasr, Camp Bucca blazed in the summer and froze in winter as fog blankets rolled in from the Persian Gulf. But it was a marked improvement on Abu Ghraib and also Camp Cropper, the facility at Baghdad International Airport reserved for the 52 regime leaders – identified on President George Bush's notorious 'deck of cards'.

Built to house 16,000 men, the camp offered medical, dental and eye care, psychiatric services, physiotherapy and more. Detainees could train in tiling, masonry, carpentry and construction; study for a high school certificate; or take courses in English, literacy and Islam. Family visits were possible. Footballs, ping-pong, Jackie Chan films, Agatha Christie mysteries and cigarettes rained down on Camp Bucca, as if from a shattered piñata.

Prisoners were streamed into two categories: enemy prisoners of war (EPW), including members of the banned Baath Party and paramilitary Fedayeen; and 'unlawful combatants', which covered everybody else from hard-core militants to innocent bystanders rounded up in the vicinity of any terrorist attack. EPWs were kept separate from non-military detainees, and Sunnis from Shia, but no more thorough documentation was possible due to the shortage of trained Arabic speakers.[2]

Other categories emerged after detainees had spent more time in the facility, and were defined by the colour of jumpsuit they wore. 'If I remember correctly,' a fighter told *The Guardian*, 'red was for people who had done things wrong while in prison, white was a prison chief, green was for a long sentence, and yellow and orange were normal.'[3]

'Even if they turn the place into a paradise,' said one detainee, 'it is still a prison full of innocent men.'[4] A Red Cross report in May 2004 stipulated that 90 per cent of detainees had been mistakenly arrested while, even in the thick of the civil war in 2007, the camp held less than 2,000 hardened insurgents, according to a survey by the camp commander, Maj. Gen. Douglas Stone. Most of its 26,000 detainees, he said, had joined the insurgency through lack or work or because of low-paying jobs.[5]

Within two weeks of Col. Brown's pep-talk to journalists, US military police had shot to death four detainees and wounded six more after a search for contraband started a riot in which 10,000 men attacked them with rocks, water bottles filled with sand and javelins made of tent poles. Two months later, they uncovered a 357-foot tunnel hours before prisoners planned to escape under cover of the fog.

The riots set the tone. Realising they could control the perimeter but not what went on inside, the authorities relinquished control to an elite of elected 'mayors', whose job it was to keep order and inform guards of planned escapes or riots. Radicals moved into the vacuum, where as *emirs* or 'princes' they ruled over compounds of up to 1,000 men, enforcing their diktat through an extreme version of Sharia law, known as *takfiri*. Improvised courts could order the slitting of tongues and gouging of eyes for those judged 'apostate', notably the more moderate prisoners.[6]

The camp authorities overlooked such incidents for the sake of tranquillity, but also sent prisoners to the '*takfiri* camp' as punishment. Imad Manhal Sultan lost his sight and part of his tongue after a four-minute assault during his three-month detention. 'The Americans send those they want dead to extremist camps [...] they passed information that I was a lawyer working for the court in Baghdad. That would make me [the detainees'] enemy since the court issues unjust verdicts against detainees.'[7]

With tacit US approval, the *emirs* transformed Camp Bucca into a vast centre of indoctrination and training – a 'jihadi university' – for the 100,000 detainees forced to live there between 2004 and 2009. Doubly imprisoned by the *takfiri*, moderate Iraqis were subjected to a reign of terror and rigorous courses of Islamist study, with no possible means of escape. 'Extremists had freedom to educate the young detainees,' said a former prisoner. 'I saw them giving courses using classroom boards on how to use explosives, weapons and how to become suicide bombers.'[8]

Most of those interned when Maj. Gen. Stone was in command were married with children, irregular mosque-goers and many admitted to drinking alcohol. After spending the average 330 days in Camp Bucca, they returned to their homes deeply traumatised men.[9]

'We could never have all got together like this in Baghdad, or anywhere else,' recalled Abu Ahmed, who was detained in 2004. 'It would have been impossibly dangerous. Here, we were not only safe, but we were only a few hundred metres away from the entire Al Qaeda leadership'.[10]

*   *   *

The future caliph of the Islamic State, Ibrahim ibn Awwad al-Badri al-Samarrai – Abu Bakr was only a *nom de guerre* – entered the proselytising furnace of Camp Bucca in its early days, though whether he was radicalised there, or before he arrived in, is open to question. Allegedly arrested in Fallujah in February 2004, he was released in December as a person of low risk, according to a Pentagon official, who said: 'He was a street thug when we picked him up.'[11]

The only contemporary photo, circulated after Abu Bakr announced his caliphate in Mosul 10 years later, is a prison shot of a jowly, unshaved man taken after in-processing or interrogation. The Pentagon description of his activities does not match those by his friends and associates in Baghdad, where Abu Bakr moved in 1989 to study Islamic law and education at the Islamic University. Polite, short-sighted, erudite, a keen footballer, they recalled.[12]

Colonel Kenneth King, who commanded Camp Bucca from 2008 till its closure a year later, said Abu Bakr was 'a bad dude, but he wasn't one of the worst.' He remembered his parting comment before flying out of Camp Bucca to Baghdad after his release – 'see you in New York' – which gave one newspaper an excuse for a most hair-raising headline.[13] That was in summer 2009, according to King: Abu Bakr was in Camp Bucca for five years, not 10 months, as the Pentagon official claimed and the caliph's public relations machine also suggested.

The discrepancy is intriguing, given the military's reputation for paperwork, as is the lack of more detailed information, despite the rigours of interrogation. This could be partly explained by the ensuing political embarrassment were Abu Bakr's release to have been approved during the Obama administration or – as was the case – under a 2008 agreement with the Iraqi government on the transfer of US-held prisoners, when President George Bush was still in office.

But partly, also, by the light more revelations would shine on the sadistic symbiosis that existed in Camp Bucca between Al Qaeda's *emirs* and US military police. 'He was respected very much by the US army,' said Abu Ahmed, an admirer of the caliph's charisma and aloofness when they were together in Camp Bucca. 'If he wanted to visit other people in the camp, he could, but we couldn't.'[14]

Hisham al-Hashimi, an Iraqi military analyst and expert on the Islamic State, insists that Abu Bakr remained for five years in US custody, saying: 'The Americans never knew who they had.'[15] If that were true, Abu Bakr had plenty of time to qualify as a trusted *emir* and build the network of Iraqi army and intelligence officers similarly interned in Camp Bucca, who planned and executed the campaigns that shot the Islamic State to power. But not to accomplish the many other tasks that the caliph's official biographer claims for him in an all-too-brief synopsis, titled *Moments from the Life Journey of our Master, the Emir of the Believers*.[16]

The unknown author mentions Baghdadi's eight-and-a-half years' experience as a jihadi, his service on the Sharia Committees of Jaysh Ahl al-Sinnah wal Jama'a (JASW), a Sunni group he reportedly founded, and on the Mujahideen Shura Council (MSC), which the JASW joined in January 2006. The MSC would mutate into the Islamic State of Iraq (ISI) later in the year. As for Camp Bucca, the biographer deals with it briskly: 'He incited for fighting and roamed and fought. He was captured and escaped.'

Moments from the Life Journey was published in mid-2013, shortly after the forerunner organisation to the Islamic State broke with Al Qaeda. It was a defensive document, seeking to rebuff those who 'slander with tongues of iron', but also to construct a pedigree for a prince who would take the momentous step a year later of declaring himself head of a caliphate, the legal and territorial manifestation of God's rule on earth.

Abu Bakr, accordingly, is described as being of the Bu Badri tribe from Samarra, descended from the Quraysh tribe of the Prophet Mohammed, which gave birth to the Umayyad, Abbasid and Fatimid Caliphates. His brothers, uncles and grandfather are all Salafist preachers or teachers of eloquence and logic; his mother supports the promotion of virtue and the prohibition of vice.

Abu Bakr's name also undergoes multiple transformations. The biographer refers to him as Dr Abu Du'a, or Ibrahim bin 'Awad bin Ibrahim al-Badri al-Radhwi al-Husseini al-Samarra'i,[17] while his spokesman, a Syrian veteran of Camp Bucca, adds 'al-Qurayshi' as a signifier of Abu Bakr's right to assume the title and status originated by the Prophet Mohammed.[18] The name – or connotation – 'al-Baghdadi' is dropped from his new title.

Abu Bakr's more intimate detractors – and there were two in his circle who broke away to rejoin Al Qaeda after the divorce – regarded this spiritual king-making as pure humbug. @ Wikibaghdady, who began tweeting his insider account in December 2013, was more worried by the Baathist officers who dictated Abu Bakr's every move, but conceded that he 'has a fake nickname and title [...] there isn't a member of al-Baghdadi's inner circle with a real name.'[19]

Abu Sulayman al-Utaybi, a Sharia scholar and former head of the Al Qaeda in Iraq (AQI) legal department, shredded Abu Bakr's resume in a measured diatribe in April 2014 that ran out of numbers after paragraph 173. He was not from Baghdad, not a doctor of Sharia, not a member of the Bu Badri tribe, and certainly not a descendant of the Quraysh. 'He ran away from Iraq at the start of the American invasion, lived in Damascus in Sayyida Zaynab [a Shia area], and stayed there for three years until 2006 [...] These three years were the years of recruiting informers.'[20]

At the time of his detention, al-Utaybi continued, Abu Bakr was responsible for an AQI dead-letter drop that US forces uncovered during the hunt for Abu Omar al-Baghdadi, AQI's first caliph, and his Egyptian military commander, Abu Ayyub al-Masri, both killed in a US air raid in April 2010. 'After leaving prison (of course, it was not a long period because [Abu Bakr] knows no one and no one knows him), he joined the [Islamic] State again.'

These different accounts demonstrate how little confidence can be placed in any description of Abu Bakr's origins, biography and gifts. But whether he is a fraud, a dupe or a military genius, the one point all agree on is that he is, at least, an Iraqi: that was a breakthrough for AQI which, in spite of its name, had always been controlled by foreigners.

2

Zarqawi's War

In January 2004 – around the time Abu Bakr was detained in Fallujah – intelligence agents from the autonomous region of Iraqi Kurdistan intercepted a letter allegedly sent by Musab al-Zarqawi to Osama bin Laden. Al-Zarqawi had been looked after by a Kurdish Salafist group, Ansar al-Islam, after crossing from Iran into northern Iraq in mid-2002, and regarded his contacts there as reliable intermediaries.

The letter is written with the chilling clarity of a psychopath. He expresses fear of a Shia state, stretching across Iran, Iraq, Syria and Lebanon, and mocks the commitment of local fighters: 'Jihad here unfortunately [takes the form of] mines planted, rockets launched and mortar shelling from afar. The Iraqi brothers still prefer safety and returning to the arms of their wives where nothing frightens them.'[1]

Under 'Work Plan', he lists – and dismisses – the danger posed by the USA, the Kurds and the New Iraq Army in 2004, and then rounds on the Shia: 'The insurmountable obstacle, the lurking snake, the crafty and malicious scorpion, the spying enemy and the penetrating venom.'[2]

'Targeting and striking their religious, political and military symbols will make them show their rage against the Sunnis and bear their inner vengeance. If we succeed in dragging them into a sectarian war, this will awaken the sleepy Sunnis.'[3] The Coalition Provisional Authority's programme of de-Baathification had converted Iraq's army, police and intelligence forces into Shia institutions: al-Zarqawi was effectively proposing that

Iraqi Sunnis should rediscover their religious purity through a campaign of collective suicide.

A few months before the letter was found, al-Zarqawi had launched his insurgency with a string of super-charged attacks that transformed the US narrative of a liberated, Saddam Hussein-free Iraq on the path to reinvention, while shoving the country sharply in the direction of civil war. The first car bomb since the US invasion exploded outside the Jordanian Embassy in Baghdad on 7 August 2003, killing or wounding 75 Iraqis who were queuing for consular services. Twelve days later, on 19 August 2003, a truck bomb struck the United Nations building, killing the special representative and 21 others. Ten days after that, two car bombs were detonated outside the Imam Ali Mosque in Najaf, 160km south of Baghdad, killing 124 worshippers and Ayatollah Mohammed Baqir al-Hakim, the spiritual leader of the Supreme Council of the Islamic Revolution in Iraq.

Each bomb was more powerful than the last, and each was directed against a specific constituency: the Hashemite Kingdom of Jordan and other US allies in the Middle East; non-government agencies and their employees seeking to alleviate post-war conditions; and the majority Shia, rapidly replacing Sunnis in key government and military positions.

Al-Zarqawi developed his visceral hatred of the Shia under the influence of a Salafist ideologue, Muhammad al-Maqdisi, with whom he founded Bayat al-Imam in 1992, but it hardened while al-Zarqawi was in Amman's al-Sawaqa prison, whose inmate elite, as in Camp Bucca, was made up of *takfiri*. Amnestied in 1999, al-Zarqawi returned to Afghanistan where he had first encountered Osama bin Laden a decade earlier.

The sheikh and the convict had little in common: bin Laden's overarching priority was the 'far enemy' – the United States, which protected corrupt, apostate regimes from Morocco to

Saudi Arabia – while al-Zarqawi argued that the 'near enemy' – the Arab regimes themselves – was a more pressing and vulnerable target. At the urging of Saif al-Adel, his Egyptian security chief, bin Laden nevertheless agreed to fund a training camp near Herat, where al-Zarqawi drilled volunteers from Jordan, Syria, Lebanon and Palestine, who crossed into western Afghanistan from Iran.[4] Bayat al-Imam, the group al-Zarqawi had founded with al-Maqdisi in the 1990s, now morphed into Jund al-Sham ('Soldiers of the Levant'), before crystallising as Al-Tawhid wal-Jihad ('Monotheism and Jihad') on his arrival in Iraq in 2002.

Little is clear-cut with al-Zarqawi. There is no evidence that he ever had real combat experience prior to moving to Iraq in 2002 and, though his name was linked to many plots before, every project he became associated with was doomed to fail – except for the assassination of a USAID civilian in 2002, which he had subcontracted to Ansar al-Islam.[5] A vociferous foe of Shiism, he nevertheless took refuge in Iran for 14 months after the US invasion as a guest of the Iranian Revolutionary Guard – whose objectives in US-occupied Iraq would ultimately, and opaquely, mesh with his own.[6]

In fact al-Zarqawi spent more time in prison than fighting in Iraq, and yet from 2003–06 he built from scratch a vast network of combat cells, spying units, safe houses, weapons caches, factories making improvised explosive devices (IEDs), suicide bombers, vest fabricators, media professionals, drivers, mechanics and a logistical system that furnished food, arms, munitions, wages, spiritual guidance, medical care and pensions for martyrs' dependants. With nothing more advanced than a mobile phone, a contacts book and word of mouth, we are led to believe, al-Zarqawi created the template for organising an urban guerrilla struggle that will be replicated and studied for years to come.

Iraq after the fall of Saddam Hussein was begging for insurgency. Hundreds of thousands of Sunnis had been expelled from the security forces and the country was awash with the arms, ammunition and explosives pillaged in the upheaval that followed invasion. Humiliated by defeat, the ever-present US convoys and patrols, unemployment and rising Shia power, the Sunni made use of their no-longer-wanted skills by embracing one of the dozens of insurgent groups that had sprouted in the Sunni Triangle, an area bound by the Tigris and Euphrates rivers that includes the governorates of Anbar, Salahuddin, Diyala and western Baghdad. The groups were organised along political, religious, tribal and familiar lines, and dissolved the differences that had once divided Islamist from Baathist – a reconciliation bin Laden broadly encouraged in a message to Iraqis on the eve of invasion, citing a seventh-century precedent.[7]

Two factors enabled al-Zarqawi to define the form and direction the insurgency was to take, giving his organisation an immediate advantage over the native resistance. The first was the indiscriminate violence of his campaign, which depended on an inexhaustible stream of foreign volunteers to perform as suicide bombers. Early estimates of the number of non-Iraqi fighters varied between the 'low hundreds' and 3,000 in 2003.[8] In May that year, al-Zarqawi met in Tehran with Saif al-Adel, who asked him to organise a network for the safe conduct of foreign fighters over the Syrian border into Iraq,[9] a task al-Zarqawi entrusted to Dr Suleiman Khaled Darwish, his chief lieutenant in the Herat camp, also known as Abu Ghadiya.[10]

Under the protection of Assef Shawkat, Syria's Director of Military Intelligence and brother-in-law of President Bashar al-Assad, Abu Ghadiya supervised a flow of foreign fighters across the 115-mile border with Iraq, notably at Sinjar and al-Qaim, which was halted only after his death in a US

Special Forces operation in 2008.[11] After successfully crossing, volunteers would make their way to staging areas via safe houses in towns along the Tigris or Euphrates rivers.

Of the 595 foreign fighters who made the journey between August 2006 and August 2007, according to the 'Sinjar Records', a cache of files captured in October 2007, 41 per cent came from Saudi Arabia, 18.8 per cent from Libya and 8.2 per cent from Syria.[12] Two years later, with the flow continuing, General David Petraeus, commander of US forces, predicted: 'In time, these fighters will turn on their Syrian hosts, and begin conducting attacks against Bashar al-Assad's regime itself.'[13]

The second key to al-Zarqawi's war was to find a means of transmitting its brutality, without censorship, to a United States in the midst of the 2004 presidential election and a Muslim audience dazzled at the prospects of nearby jihad. In May, a masked militant, later identified, but not confirmed, as al-Zarqawi, was filmed sawing off the head of an abducted American, Nicholas Berg, and placing it on his torso amid the hosannas of his comrades. Mimicking the decapitation of journalist Daniel Pearl in Pakistan two years earlier by Khaled Sheikh Mohammed, architect of the plan to destroy the New York World Trade Center, a 5- and-1/2-minute video of Berg's murder was posted on the al-AnsarWeb internet forum, from where it was downloaded millions of times.[14]

Coinciding with breakthrough developments in bandwidth, video compression and editing, al-Zarqawi's insurgency broadcast unfiltered footage of executions, combat engage-ments, the emplacement and detonation of (IEDs), political rants, religious sermons and daily operational updates. Abu Maysara al-Iraqi, a Syrian despite his nickname, was appointed webmaster in June 2004, and took producer credit on the hour-long 'Winds of Victory' feature about foreign suicide bombers, relaxing, writing their wills and finally exploding 'from multiple angles'.[15] Although Abu Maysara was detained during the second battle of Fallujah in November 2004, al-Zarqawi's media team still posted nine online statements a day.

But al-Zarqawi's media operations were a double-edged sword. On the positive side, they acted as a 'force multiplier' by convincing viewers – including Western journalists – that his organisation was a much greater threat than it was: the State Department concluded that it represented only 10–12 per cent of the active insurgency in 2005.[16] On the down side, al-Zarqawi's high profile played into enemy hands, according to documents leaked in 2006, which described a US propaganda operation using local media to fan hostility to al-Zarqawi by accenting his non-Iraqi origins, an outcome that his webcasts served to reinforce.[17] Osama bin Laden's deputy, Ayman al-Zawahiri, raised the issue in a reproving letter to al-Zarqawi in July 2005. 'Can the assumption of leadership [...] by non-Iraqis stir up sensitivity for some people? And if there is sensitivity, what is its effect?'

Bandwidth was one thing; brand loyalty quite another. Although the media shorthand of 'Al Qaeda in Iraq' had eclipsed Al-Tawhid wal-Jihad as the usual attribution for al-Zarqawi's attacks, the relationship between al-Zarqawi and bin Laden's versions of Al Qaeda was shaky, and the old name lingered. 'Renowned for his imprudence and passion,' as Saif al-Adel described him,[18] al-Zarqawi was also morbidly petulant. In theory, the US invasion was an opportunity to engage the near and the far enemy simultaneously, so ending any doctrinal dispute between the two leaders, but al-Zarqawi's campaign of assassinations, kidnappings and bomb attacks against civilians conflicted with Al Qaeda's strict non-aggression pact with non-Sunni actors, notably Iran, where it benefited from strategic depth and refuge for family members.[19]

Even as negotiations were underway for a more formal association between the networks, al-Zarqawi approved two complex attacks, involving gunmen, suicide bombers and car bombs, on the Day of Ashura on 2 March 2004, killing 180 pilgrims in Karbala and Baghdad. Still, each needed the other's reflected glow: bin Laden, to retain relevance in the global jihad, then focusing on Iraq; and al-Zarqawi, to increase his finances and recruitment under Al Qaeda's banner. After eight months of talks, al-Zarqawi swore his allegiance to the 'mujahid commander' on 17 October, adopting the new title of *emir* of 'Al Qaeda in Iraq' (AQI), but it was a marriage in name only. A month earlier, he declared all-out war on Shias after the loss of 837 killed or captured insurgents in a US–Iraqi offensive in Tal Afar, Ninewa province,[20] and in an otherwise obsequious online announcement al-Zarqawi called bin Laden a 'fine commander [...] against the inveterate infidels and apostates'.[21]

The dispute over al-Zarqawi's sectarian war continued into 2005 as total attacks increased by 29 per cent to an average of 90 per day, but car bombs and suicide bombings – the weapons most commonly used in indiscriminate, mass-casualty incidents – rose by 209 per cent and 857 per cent, respectively. While the number of US military dead remained steady at 71 per month during the same period, Iraqi civilians died at a rate of 750 per month in early 2004, compared to 1,800 per month in late 2005.[22] Al-Zawahiri tried to restrain him in yet another intercepted letter written in July 2005, which Al Qaeda later repudiated as a forgery. In it he lays out Al Qaeda's four goals in Iraq: 1) expel the Americans; 2) establish an Islamic emirate [...] to fill the void stemming from the Americans' departure; 3) extend the jihad to secular countries neighbouring Iraq; and 4) ... the clash with Israel.

He writes of how al-Zarqawi's war against the Shia was damaging the reputation of Islam. 'Among the things which the feelings of the Muslim populace who love and support you will never find palatable are the scenes of slaughtering the hostages. You shouldn't be deceived by the praise of some of the jealous young men and their description of you as the "sheikh of the slaughterers". And in what appears to be an oblique reference to the Holocaust, he wonders: 'Can the mujahideen kill all the Shia in Iraq? Has any Islamic state in history ever tried that?'[23] A year earlier Muhammad al-Maqdisi, al-Zarqawi's former mentor, had also criticised his pupil's definition of Shia as apostates, and repeated that targeting innocent civilians and their mosques was counter-productive.[24]

But Saif al-Adel was surprisingly upbeat about his comrade's modus operandi. He speculated that the expansion of the violence in Iraq to Syria and Lebanon would bring the Islamist movement close 'to the border of occupied Palestine' and into direct confrontation with Israel, further legitimising the jihadist cause.[25]

In mid-May 2011, Saif al-Adel was appointed interim *emir* of Al Qaeda, after the killing of Osama bin Laden in Abbottabad, Pakistan. Al-Zawahiri, the organisation's spiritual head, would continue to 'monitor international contacts', but al-Adel would be responsible for command and control.[26]

3

The First Caliph

Al-Zarqawi's goal of creating a pure Islamic state in Iraq left no room for nuance in his relations with the indigenous Sunni resistance, particularly the Islamic Army in Iraq (IAI) and the Mujahideen Army (MA), which represented half the insurgency.[1] Despite their Islamist names, these Baghdad-oriented organisations were as much Baathist and tribal, driven less by bigotry than fears of Iranian domination of the Shia government that emerged after Sunni parties boycotted the elections in January 2005.

AQI's attacks against US forces, the Iraqi Security Forces (ISF) and Shia militias were a welcome complement to their own efforts, but the mass killing of Shia civilians was a line they refused to cross: reconciliation was in the air as they negotiated Sunni re-admission to the political process before the national elections in December. In June, the IAI and MA explored the options for disarmament and a truce with the government, while a clash between IAI and AQI in October indicated a growing disconnect between the domestic and international insurgencies.[2]

Stirrings of discontent were particularly audible in Anbar, the sparsely populated province reaching all the way from Baghdad to the Syrian border. In June US soldiers captured AQI's *emir* in Mosul,[3] and US and Iraqi forces aggressively cleared AQI from the occupied towns of Qusaybah, Karabila, Sada, Al-Qaim and Ubaydi on the Euphrates. Also linked to the looming elections, a follow-on operation was planned on the Euphrates segment from Hit to Ramadi, Anbar's capital, 70 miles west of Baghdad.

Residents of Ramadi had welcomed al-Zarqawi's fighters after Saddam Hussein fell, but dreaded a repeat of the two-month US siege of Fallujah that destroyed 36,000 buildings and displaced 90 per cent of its population by December 2004. A year later, Ramadi's tribal sheikhs met with US commanders to discuss persuading their young men to abandon the AQI if they could be trained, equipped and paid to operate as a local police force.[4] It was the first step towards the 'Anbar Awakening'.

Three months after bin Laden conferred the name-recognition al-Zarqawi desired, he was persuaded to renounce it by submerging AQI in a coalition with five unknown Sunni groups in a ploy to add protective colouring and a patina of consultation to his decision making. Officially headed by an Iraqi, the Mujahideen Shura Council's declared goal was to 'liberate Iraq from occupation, to unite and direct all mujahideen efforts',[5] but the IAI, MA and a former AQI ally, Ansar al-Sunna, refused to play along.

The MSC henceforth claimed ownership of all AQI activities, but made no important policy changes until after al-Zarqawi's death in June 2006. The new organisation did mark the public debut of Abu Bakr al-Baghdadi, the future head of ISIS and the Islamic State. His Fallujah-based group, Jaysh Ahl al-Sinnah wal Jama'a, became the seventh partner in the coalition on 30 January 2006, entitling Abu Bakr to a seat on the council, but not a public profile.[6]

The destruction of the Al-Askari Mosque in Samarra three weeks later, on 22 February 2006, sparked the sectarian conflagration that al-Zarqawi craved, but the MSC curiously did not take credit for it, either then or later. Some aspects of the attack, which used sophisticated explosive charges at an hour that spared hundreds of worshippers' lives, were atypical of the

AQI style; some suspected a false-flag operation by followers of Saddam Hussein, who was then on trial for killing 148 Shia in a 1982 massacre.[7] Whoever blew up the shrine, dedicated to the 10th, 11th and 12th Imams, knew it would enflame a murderous uproar.

Tens of thousands of Shia surged into the streets, vowing retribution against Sunnis and the multinational forces, although Ayatollah Sistani, the moderate Shia leader, cautioned: 'It was not [their] Sunni neighbours who were killing them, but foreign Wahhabis.'[8] Iraqi authorities reported the deaths of 379 people in the five days that followed the bombing, and scores of tit-for-tat attacks against mosques and shrines. By contrast, Ellen Knickmeyer of the *Washington Post* found evidence that over 1,000 bodies had been admitted to Baghdad morgues in just two days, claims that were verified when Wikileaks released eyewitness accounts by US military personnel at the scene.[9]

The post-Askari killings, however, were merely a spike in a pattern of sectarian murders by Shia death squads under orders from Interior Minister, Bayan Jabr. John Pace, head of the UN Human Rights body in Iraq, said that Baghdad's central morgue had received 1,100 bodies in July 2005 alone, of which 900 bore signs of torture or summary execution.[10]

The impact of this trend could be graphically seen in Baghdad as death squads from both sides worked to empty their neighbourhoods of the weaker sect. In 2003, most neighbourhoods were mixed, but Sunnis predominated in Hurriya, Washash, Mansur, Khark, Sadiya and Adhamiya. After the Al-Askari bombing, sectarian killings peaked at 3,462 in November 2006: Sadiya, Washash and Hurriya changed from Sunni to Shia areas, while Amiriya and Ghazaliya went in the opposite direction. By mid-2007, sectarian cleansing of the capital was almost complete, and only central Baghdad still had large mixed areas. Sunnis also made up the largest share of the 2 million Iraqi refugees in Syria and Jordan, and the 1.7 million internally displaced.[11]

Musab al-Zarqawi died on 7 June 2006 after being hit by two 500-pound bombs at a meeting with his spiritual advisor, Sheikh Abd al-Rahman, in a village near Baquba, north of Baghdad. He survived for an hour after the impact.[12] Clues to his whereabouts allegedly came from two sources: al-Rahman, whose movements were tracked over a six-week period; and Jordanian intelligence, still furious over attacks on three high-end Amman hotels the previous November. Even bin Laden was happy to see him go: 'He had clear instructions,' he said in a video eulogy, 'to focus his combat against the occupying aggressors, especially the Americans, and to treat as neutral all those who wanted to be neutral.'[13]

His successor was Abu Ayyub al-Masri, a confidant of al-Zawahiri, supervisor of AQI's bomb-making trainees and, crucially, a safe pair of hands in time of transition. Al-Masri's lasting contribution to the AQI – and the organisations that followed it – was to place it on a robust bureaucratic footing in readiness for the declaration of a caliphate.[14] Al-Zawahiri believed that the Iraqi jihad would end in 'killing, ruin and destruction', as it had in Afghanistan after the collapse of the Soviet-backed regime, unless rigid managerial and accounting procedures were established.[15]

Al-Masri introduced pay records, personnel files, membership forms, regular cell meetings and operational after-action reports to the loose network of semi-independent cells al-Zarqawi had created, with a consequent loss of creative agility in the core business of killing. Bookkeeping was orderly to the point of being pedantic after 2006. As one AQI member complained in a captured memo:

The number of *emirs* increased and every speciality began having its own *emir*, such as the *Emir* of Mortars, *Emir* of Administration, *Emir* of Booby-traps, *Emir* of Support, *Emir* of Gas, *Emir* of Tents, *Emir* of Kitchen and the General *Emir*, and his Deputy, and others that were the reason behind the cessation of reverence from the hearts of the brothers toward their *Emirs*.[16]

Al-Masri was Egyptian and thus disqualified from leading an AQI that purported to represent Iraqis, but al-Zarqawi's campaign had been so virulent that no other candidate was available to stand. The solution was an individual with no verifiable history or place of origin, called Abu Omar al-Baghdadi, another pseudonym. Abu Sulayman al-Utaybi, the Saudi judge who quit the Islamic State in disgust, remembered him as 'a normal person and not a leader'.[17] He might have been a junior member of the MSC, as Al Qaeda claimed; a dismissed army officer with extremist views, according to Iraqi intelligence;[18] or a mouthpiece, played by a professional actor, Abu Abdullah al-Naima, as US intelligence wanted people to believe.[19] If the former, he had no profile whatsoever; if the last, he remained faithful to al-Zarqawi's script.

A few days after al-Zarqawi's death, a video was posted of al-Baghdadi recommitting the MSC to the destruction of Shias, followed by footage of the beheading of four Russian diplomats on 21 June 2006.[20] In mid-October, an MSC spokesman announced the creation of the Islamic State of Iraq (ISI), a shadow government covering Sunni territories in Anbar, Diyala, Kirkuk, Salahuddin, Ninewa and parts of Babel and al-Wassat governorates, with a capital in Baquba, Diyala province. Abu Omar al-Baghdadi was appointed caliph of this unsecured domain.

The declaration of an Islamic state, ruled by a non-entity, was a crucial misreading of Iraqi culture and events on the ground, at once an insult to the home-grown insurgency and a threat to the tribal sheikhs. Even as AQI reached the apex of its territorial control, the ground had began to shift beneath its feet.

At least 75 per cent of Iraqis identify with one of the country's 150 tribes, whatever other networks – Islamist, Baathist, military, business or criminal – accrued outside the kinship framework.[21] A tribal sheikh was very much like a warlord, though draped with more genealogy. The 2003 invasion had ended the informal treaties that ensured tribal loyalty to Saddam Hussein, in exchange for autonomy in security, judicial affairs and the economic favours that reinforced the sheikh's prestige and made tribal identity a viable social and business model. Cut adrift, the Anbar sheikhs threw in with the insurgency, rather than the invading army, particularly AQI's forerunner, which relied on the supply of fighters from Syria along the Tigris and Euphrates valleys. This venture required safe houses, logistical experience, inside knowledge, manpower and was paid in cash, but the cost finally outweighed the benefits.

AQI militants made very bad guests. They kidnapped dignitaries with impunity, assassinated tribal and religious leaders and anyone in the local police, commandeered homes, farms and even women for the insurgency's use. AQI further enflamed local opinion by banning customs, such as the worship of saints, and replacing the sheikh's flexible justice with Sharia courts, presided over by Salafists, often Saudis. In Diyala, courts ordered beatings for men who smoked, wore jewellery, shaved or sold food to 'apostates', and amputation or beheading for more serious infractions.[22]

Able-bodied tribesmen outnumbered the AQI, even at the highest estimate, by at least 50 to one, but the latter's firepower, discipline and guerrilla skills made for an unequal contest. The Albu Mahal, who live on both sides of the Iraq–Syria border, had turned their guns on AQI in 2005 after it took over their smuggling operations, but the uprising faltered after heavy losses.[23] Another attempt by the Anbar People's Council ended with over half of its leadership being assassinated.[24] In August 2006, AQI had murdered Sheikh Abu Ali Jassim for encouraging people to join the police, hiding his body in a field rather than returning it to the family for burial.[25]

Sheikh Abdul Sattar of the Abu Risha, exiled to Amman, had seen his wealth dry up, and his father and three brothers killed, as AQI usurped his traditional livelihoods – levying taxes on the Amman–Baghdad highway and smuggling oil products from the Baiji refinery.[26] In September 2006 he returned to Ramadi and formed an alliance with 17 sheikhs to expel AQI from Anbar and encourage tribesmen to join the Ramadi branch of the Shia-controlled police force, then numbering just 300 officers. More than 4,500 signed up within three months and, by 2008, Anbar boasted 24,000 Sunni police, armed, trained and paid for by Multi-National Force – Iraq (MNF–I).[27]

The Anbar Awakening, *Sahwa* or Sons of Iraq, as Abdul Sattar's initiative was variously called, was no naïf tribal rallying behind the US-led coalition or Iraqi nationhood, but a massive neighbourhood watch scheme, in which former tribal members of the Iraq army and the AQI were paid to guard the very same infrastructure they once sought to sabotage. *Sahwa* units were deployed to protect highways, pipelines, dams, canals and villages. But it was also a period of convulsive counter-revolution between brothers and cousins, families and gangs, from which the notion of the hierarchical 'tribe' seemed to emerge intact, while thousands of blood feuds streamed on through the years.

Despite misgivings over the threat posed by an armed Sunni militia, Prime Minister Nouri al-Maliki encouraged similar *Sahwa* formations across Iraq, restoring to the Albu Mahal its traditional right to the smuggling business across the Syrian border.[28] With such inducements, 'local committees' sprang up across Sunni Iraq – the Albu Issa in Fallujah, the Karabila in Al Qaim, the Al Zuba'a, Shammar, Jubur, Tayy, al-Nuaim, Kirkeah, Albu Badran and even Yazidi tribes.[29] By early 2009, 91,000 Sunni tribesmen, grouped in 130 *Sahwa* councils, were on the MNF–I payroll at wages of $300 per month in US currency.[30]

4

Clear, Hold and Build

The surge in US forces, announced in January 2007, would never have succeeded to the degree it did without the eyes, ears and intelligence of the *Sahwa*, who had loaned the same faculties to AQI, or the Islamic State of Iraq (ISI), as it had now become. On the other hand, the knowledge which the tribes have of the local terrain, and their previous experience with the insurgency it now intended to betray, would not have been leveraged without an intermediary strong enough to interpose between them, the Shia government and the ISI.

The ISI reacted to the challenge by stepping up attacks on police stations, checkpoints, policemen and their families – increasingly Sunni as the year wore on – and a stinging denunciation of *Sahwa* treachery. 'Oh armies of God [...],' urged Abu Omar al-Baghdadi, 'eradicate this noxious bacteria and purify the world [...] use any force and pressure and tear apart their limbs, demolish their houses and burn their property.'[1]

One aspect of ISI's response stood out: the first use of chlorine as an improvised chemical weapon. The earliest attack in Ramadi involved a truck bomb laden with mortar shells and chlorine, but the temperature of the explosives neutralised the chemical's impact.[2] A second attempt took place in January 2007 when a suicide bomber drove a chlorine vehicle-bomb into a Ramadi police base, killing 16.[3]

The US plan for defeating the insurgency – 'Clear, Hold and Build' – became the template for all counter-insurgency operations in Anbar over the next 12 months. First, mount checkpoints on all roads to isolate ISI from re-supply and reinforcement; second, build barriers between neighbourhoods, and sweep for insurgents and weapons; third, construct combat outposts and construct police stations, manned by Sunnis; and, lastly, remove 'reconcilable' elements from the insurgency by creating jobs with discretionary funds under the Commander Emergency Response Program (CERPs) or the government's reconstruction budget. 'Money is the most powerful ammunition we have,' said Major General David Petraeus in 2003, when testing this methodology in Mosul as commander of the 101st Airborne.[4]

In January 2007 President Bush announced that an additional 20,000 troops would be sent to Iraq and mid-tour leave was cancelled for the 150,000 US troops already there. The largest part, 17,500 US combat troops, was imbedded with Iraqi Security Forces (ISF) units at 100 locations across Baghdad to secure neighbourhoods already cleared of insurgents, while 4,000 Marines were deployed in Anbar province. General David Petraeus was named commander of Multi-National Force – Iraq (MNF–I) under the same presidential order.

By February 2007, the MNF–I/ISF had cleared Ramadi, Fallujah and other cities, pushing ISI fighters into western Baghdad or north into Diyala province. Violent incidents in Anbar fell from 300–400 per week to nearly zero per week by the spring.[5] Ramadi was one of a number of 'shaping' operations, aimed at disrupting the insurgents' freedom of movement prior to implementing Operation *Fardh Qanoon* (Imposing Law), or the Baghdad Security Plan. Similar operations were taking place in Diyala and the Baghdad Belts.

The Baghdad Belts denotes the outer ring of towns, farms and industrial areas in a radius of 20–30 miles of the capital, criss-crossed with highways, smaller roads, rivers and irrigation canals. AQI relied on the Belts' amorphous clutter as a rear base for its Baghdad campaign: fabricating IEDs, suicide vests and car bombs; storing weapons and fighters; and using its links, including the Tigris, to transport them to where they were needed. More preoccupied with halting ethnic cleansing inside the city, US forces had 'not been there in a long time'.[6]

In 2006, US soldiers had found a crude map in black felt-tip on al-Zarqawi's corpse, which appeared to sketch out a plan to seize areas of central Baghdad, using the Belts as a springboard for infiltrating fighters.[7] By reverse-engineering al-Zarqawi's map, the Baghdad Security Plan sought to eliminate ISI in the capital by disrupting its bases in the Belts and squeezing its urban units into ever shrinking corners of operation.

Operation Phantom Thunder, launched on 15 June 2007, was the largest military offensive since the invasion and – with the Anbar Awakening – another beginning-of-the-end moment for the ISI's first attempt to establish an Islamic state in Iraq. A traditional hammer-and-anvil tactic, Phantom Thunder's goal was to use the surge's additional strength to block every access point into the capital on two concentric circles around Baghdad: one, 15–30 miles distant from the city; the second, on its immediate circumference.[8]

While this was going on, support operations were underway in known ISI safe havens in the Belts – Arab Jabour and Salman Pak in the south-east, Mahmudiyah in the south-west – but also in strongholds as far away as Hilla, Baquba, Fallujah, Ramadi and Lake Thar Thar. Within the cordon's inner circle, the focus was on clearing Adhamiya in the north-east, Rashid in the south and Mansour in the north-west, fault lines where most of the sectarian violence took place.

Confronted by a force of 74,000, supported by the full panoply of war, the ISI, Sadr Army and other anti-government groups had no choice but step aside, or perish. When Operation Phantom Thunder ended on 13 August 2007, the

MNF–I said it had killed 1,196 militants, killed or captured 382 high-value targets, detained 6,700 suspects – who would lick their wounds in Camp Bucca – and neutralised 2,000 IEDs and 1,113 weapons caches.[9] Independent sources showed Shia executions of Sunnis falling from 30 a day in June to 7.4 in November; and Sunni bombings of Shia falling from 7.2 to 2.3 per day.[10] US combat deaths also tapered sharply from a high of 108 in May to 40 in November, before ebbing further in late 2008.[11]

Meanwhile, the abrasive relations ISI always entertained with Iraqi rebel groups erupted into open fighting, adding another threat to those it faced from the MNF–I and the *Sahwa*. After the ISI assassinated the leader of the 1920 Revolution Brigade in March and a dozen MA fighters two months later, the first formed a *Sahwa*-styled 'Adhamiya Awakening', while the latter joined a new coalition to coordinate a joint armed response.[12] In late May, fighting broke out between the two sides in Amiriyah, one of Baghdad's most dangerous districts, and lasted for several days. 'It is no longer acceptable what these people are doing to our Sunni neighbourhoods,' said an Iraqi insurgent commander. 'They're ghost towns where nobody can live. That's why it came to a fight.'[13]

The shaping operations begun in Diyala in early March culminated in mid-June 2007 with the launch of Operation Arrowhead Ripper, a joint operation to clear Baquba, the acting capital of the Islamic state. It took 10 days of street-to-street fighting by 10,000 soldiers, supported by fixed-wing and Apache aircraft, to subjugate the city, but only 55 insurgent deaths were reported – suggesting a disciplined withdrawal had taken place beneath the dust of war. The only viable direction of retreat was northwards, and since two of three routes transited Iraqi Kurdistan, insurgents had run the gauntlet along the

Tigris, now riveted with checkpoints manned by tribes in the Pentagon's pay.

Mosul offered opportunities for concealment unavailable elsewhere in Iraq by late 2007. The ISI had thrust deep roots into the Sunni areas on the west bank of the Tigris and, through alliance with Ansar al-Sunna, in Kurdish eastern Mosul. Pre-invasion, the Sunni majority played a disproportionate role in Saddam Hussein's officer corps and many had acquired property after the eviction of Kurds under a programme designed to shore up Mosul's role as sentinel at a crossroads of international pipelines, highways and borders.

The use of Kurdish *peshmerga* to recapture the city from insurgents in 2004, meanwhile, had further divided Arab and Kurd. The city's military traditions and its location, at once close to Syria but far from the capital, made it a fertile source of recruits and finance for the Iraqi insurgency and al-Zarqawi's foreign legion. Since Petraeus' time, moreover, troop levels had been repeatedly cut by requisitions from Baghdad, until only 1,000 US and 6,500 ISF were left to hold a city of 1.8 million people.[14] By early 2008, some parts of Mosul had not seen a US or Iraqi patrol in 15 months.[15]

In mid-2007 US and Iraqi forces killed or captured six *emirs*, four cell leaders and two facilitators, but the northwards withdrawal after Baquba and Baghdad enabled ISI to repair its Ninewa network and even increase the level of attacks. As a symbol of its enduring commitment to cleansing the Islamic state of heretics, it detonated five truck bombs in Qataniya and Adnaniya, villages near the Syrian border, killing more than 500 Yazidi Kurds and injuring 350 in what was described as the deadliest attack since the destruction of the World Trade Center.[16] Attacks across Ninewa increased to 80 per week in November 2007, rising to 180 per week by mid-February.[17]

In January 2008 – a year after the surge was announced – the US and ISF commanders deployed an additional 60,000 men to Ninewa in readiness for what was flagged as the decisive battle for the ISI's last stronghold. The bombing of the Ninewa police chief's car on 26 January, as he visited a site where 60 civilians had died in a bomb attack earlier in the day, seemed to suggest a more rapid response was needed, but the Mosul campaign stayed on hold until May. Twenty new combat outposts were built to support district reclamation and a berm restored to allow more effective police checkpoints. A circle of US armour was thrown round Mosul to seal it from reinforcement or retreat. On 10 May 2008, Operation Lion's Roar commenced with a 72-hour lockdown as Iraqi forces, supported by 10,000 *Sahwa*, went from street to street in the now near-deserted city, encountering suspiciously little resistance. After two weeks of operations, ISF reported the capture of 1,000 insurgents, 12 tonnes of explosives, 500 mortars and more than 200 IEDs, but a pitiably small number of deaths.[18]

As if al-Masri didn't have enough trouble, Al Qaeda's al-Zawahiri wrote asking him to respond to complaints about his leadership, which had been raised by Abu Sulayman al-Utaybi, former head of AQI's legal system. Intercepted by Coalition forces in Baghdad on 24 April 2008, one of the letters, dated 25 January 2008 – quoting al-Utaybi, as source – says al-Masri is

> totally isolated, barely seeing or being seen by anyone, except a very select few .... The reports that are sent to him from the *emirs* of the regions, districts and sectors mention only the positives and the cheerful and uplifting things, and they don't mention the negatives and the problems as they really are.[19]

The most damaging criticism touched on the root of misun-
derstanding with Al Qaeda that had existed since al-Zarqawi's
command.

'He [al-Utaybi] considers the declaration of the [Islamic]
State, in the manner with which it was declared and formed,
to have been a mistake, and that there was exaggeration (to
a degree which could be called lying) in what was said in
terms of the presence in, and support for it, among the heads
of the tribes.'[20]

5

The Successions

The US conviction that it had defeated the Islamic State of Iraq (ISI) insurgency was consistent with independent analysis that showed civilian deaths plunging from a peak of 29,000 in 2006 to 9,600 in 2008 and 4,050 by 2010.[1] The number of terrorist attacks also fell away from over 6,000 a month in 2006–07 into the low hundreds.[2]

General Ray Odierno said in June that 34 of ISI's 42 most senior leaders had been killed or captured, including the war minister, Abu Ayyub al-Masri, and his semi-fictitious caliph, Abu Omar al-Baghdadi.[3] Funds and volunteers from Syria dried up and cells were 'disintegrating into local criminal franchises', according to analyst Dr Michael Knights.[4] After seven years of ill-conceived, illegal and unpopular occupation, minimum conditions existed in 2010 for a withdrawal that could be presented to the public as an ending: not a defeat, nor a dereliction of duty and certainly not a victory.

The 'metrics' were also reassuring for the future of Iraq after US troops withdrew on 31 December 2011, in accordance with the Status of Forces Agreement (SOFA) signed in late 2008. More dismal trends were visible beneath the surface, however. Combat troops had pulled out of cities by 1 July 2009, sharply reducing the number of US targets, and sectarian killing had not been suppressed: it had halted because it had achieved its goal of partitioning Baghdad into parallel confessional districts. Despite Operation Lion's Roar and other operations to pacify the north, Mosul was more violent than Baghdad, a city five times as large.[5]

The base-line carnage continued, but at a lower intensity and without the signature flourishes that distinguished ISI's multi-target attacks from the background noise. Those that most chimed with its operational art, such as the coordinated truck and car bomb attacks on the finance and foreign affairs ministries in August 2009, and the ministry of justice and Baghdad City Council two months later, were revealed as Iranian forgeries, aimed at manufacturing the same sense of security breakdown ISI had pioneered in its heyday.[6]

Camp Bucca released its last 10,000 detainees in September 2009, before closing under the SOFA. Disagreements persisted between the US and Iraqi governments over what constituted torture, for the former, and evidence, for the latter, a process that tended to work in favour of the inmates' early release – up to 30 per cent had already been detained for three years without charge, trial or sentence.[7] Many left with an unslaked thirst for revenge against the police, *Sahwa* or civilians who had put them in Camp Bucca in the first place.[8] One Iraqi security source in 2010 estimated ISI's strength as high as 12,000 fighters, with 10,000 freelancers on call, but if that were true, where were they?[9]

The Al Qaeda 'manual' of operations advises a period of *al-tazhahur bi'l-mawt* – or 'playing dead' – in the event of a major setback on the battlefield.[10] The time ISI spent in retreat was likely devoted to regrouping and reassessing the mistakes it had made in its relationship with tribes that went so badly wrong in Anbar. 'Do not close the door of repentance against those Sunnis who turned against us,' al-Masri urged in a radio message that might be interpreted as an apology after so much invective had been hurled at them as traitors and apostates.[11] Later broadcasts ordered combatants not to interfere with 'head covering, the satellite and other social affairs, which are against our religion, until further notice'.[12]

The *Sahwa*, like the ISI, was not the unified movement it had been in 2006–08. The assassination of its founder, Sheikh Abu Risha, on 13 September 2007 drove a wedge between his brother, Ahmed, and other rivals for the leadership that created two separate tribal wings, allowing Baghdad to play one against the other in the enduring quest for patronage. After switching their loyalties from the insurgency to the counter-insurgency, the sheikhs found Prime Minister Nouri al-Maliki played by a different set of rules. Jobs were available for some, but 50,000 tribesmen were in units where pay was inconstant. 'It's an easy market for Al Qaeda now,' said Sheikh Moustafa al-Jabouri. 'The Iraqi government has disappointed them and it is an easy choice to rejoin the terrorists.'[13]

In a move that highlighted al-Maliki's indifference to reconciliation, the De-Baathification Committee banned 500 Sunni candidates from standing for office in the parliamentary elections of 2010, because of alleged associations with Saddam Hussein's one-party state. It was a declaration of war by constitutional means. Sunnis responded by voting for the Iraqi National Movement, led by Ayad Allawi, which beat al-Maliki's State of Law Coalition by two seats to become the largest bloc in parliament – triggering nine months of political gridlock. By the time the United States withdrew 15 months later, Sheikh Ahmed Abu Risha was actively campaigning for Anbar to enjoy the same autonomy as Iraqi Kurdistan, as separatists were doing in Diyala, Salahuddin and the Shia province of Basra, raising fears about the possible break-up of Iraq.[14]

The possibility of an autonomous Sunni enclave, though still a mirage in 2010, gave ISI a handhold for clambering back into the good graces of Anbar's tribes. So when Abu Ayyub al-Masri and Abu Omar al-Baghdadi were tracked down and killed in Tikrit on 18 April 2010, there was an opportunity to re-invent the ISI in a security environment cleared of US entanglements.

The new leadership, announced after a month of argument, displayed a distinctly Baathist complexion, to the dismay of @Wikibaghdady, the renegade leaker, who again wondered if the ISI had been co-opted by Iraqi or Syrian intelligence.[15]

All three members of the military council were Iraqis, veterans of Saddam Hussein's army, the Baath Party – and also Camp Bucca. Abu Muslim al-Turkmani was a former intelligence officer and Abu Abdulrahman al-Bilawi an ex-infantry captain. The war minister, replacing Abu Ayyub al-Masri, was a Moroccan, named Nasser al-Din Allah Abu Suleiman, but he deferred to Samir al-Khlifawi, the third member of the council, better known as Haji Bakr.[16]

A former colonel in the Iraqi army, Haji Bakr was 'a fox of a man (who was fed the Baath Party line and cunning at birth)'. @Wikibaghdady alleged he had rigged the election by privately assuring each delegate that all the others were in favour of Abu Bakr's appointment. 'The selection of Abu Bakr was worse than [that of] his predecessor,' he wrote, 'he was neither known to us, nor to most of the brothers, the leaders. Because of secrecy and weak communication, each person would think that so-and-so had selected him.'[17]

While re-branding the ISI as a purely Iraqi organisation, its neo-Baathist leadership allowed it to draw closer to the Sunni insurgency – partly demobilised to contest the elections as parties – without jettisoning its anti-Shia agenda, which became more beguiling as the rewards of political engagement diminished to nothing. Whether that amounted to an internal coup by senior leaders seeking to subjugate ISI's manpower and wealth to a Baathist programme of action, @Wikibaghdady infers, is impossible to ascertain. Nevertheless, Haji Bakr embarked on a campaign of assassination of dozens of militants opposed to Abu Bakr's election that was more typical of the Saddam Hussein regime than the ISI, earning him the nickname, 'Knight of the Silencers'.[18]

One possible ally of interest at this time was Jaysh Rijal al-Tariq al-Naqshbandi (JRTN), a Sufi network of army veterans, led by Saddam Hussein's red-haired, former vice-president, Izzat Ibrahim al-Douri – the King of Clubs in Bush's 'most-wanted' deck of cards. The JRTN had been formed in reaction to the hanging of Saddam Hussein in December 2006, footage of which circulated by cellphone, and was fighting to turn back the clock to the status quo that existed before his overthrow. JRTN was the only Iraqi insurgent force to have grown in strength since the US surge, and was strongly established in Mosul and Kirkuk.[19]

Haji Bakr and Abu Bakr were inseparable to the degree that 'many considered him to be al-Baghdadi's private minister'. Repairing ISI's cash flow became their pressing concern. They agreed a four-point plan: to collect taxes from the Shia, Christians and other minorities; to regain control of the Baiji oil refinery; to extort subcontractors on reconstruction projects; and to repossess the highways business that had reverted to the sheikhs during the ISI downturn. 'This led to more people wanting to join the [ISI],' wrote @Wikibaghdady, 'especially when they found out how much some members were getting paid.'[20]

Abu Bakr gave a foretaste of the style of his caliphate in November 2010 when suicide bombers took hostage the entire congregation of Our Lady of Deliverance Church in Baghdad in pretend outrage at the imprisonment in Egypt of a woman – a convert to Islam – by Coptic Christians. 'They were well trained,' said a witness, 'they didn't say anything. It was like someone had cut out their tongues.' When Iraqi forces stormed the building, the bombers detonated their vests which were filled with ball bearings, killing 50 Assyrian Christians and wounding 70 others.[21] It was the first, mass-casualty attack against non-Muslims since the Yazidi massacre in Ninewa in August 2007.

But Abu Bakr's hold on power was less than secure. When hundreds of thousands of Syrians took to the streets the following March, the high-water mark of the Arab Spring revolts, his battle-weary militants drifted away to the gentler jihad arising in Al-Sham, fertile heartland of the original caliphates. As desertions increased, he ordered one of his most trusted lieutenants, Abu Muhammad al-Julani, to select a core group of fighters and facilitators to take to Syria and establish new cells loyal to the ISI and its leader.[22]

Al-Julani was a 39-year-old Syrian, originally from the Golan Heights, who joined AQI under al-Zarqawi, and may have had links with him dating from his years in Afghanistan. Precious little was known of him before 2014 when a rash of details emerged after his first filmed interview with Al Jazeera's Tayseer Allouni, a fellow Syrian and former prisoner himself.

Allegedly detained in Camp Bucca from 2006–08, al-Julani was appointed the ISI *emir* in 'Mosul province' on his release. As a Syrian, he had inside knowledge of the pipeline of foreign fighters organised by al-Zarqawi, and a clear understanding of the revolutionary ideas of Abu Musab al-Suri, a jihadi theorist from Aleppo. Back in his native land with his own command after so many years in exile, al-Julani set about creating a style of leadership very different from that of the man who had sent him.[23]

6

Springtime for Qatar

When the suicide of a Tunisian fruit vendor in December 2010 inspired a wave of protest that unseated three North African despots and sent shockwaves across the Middle East, nobody was more taken aback than the movement for global jihad. Peaceful protest had achieved in weeks what organised terrorism failed to deliver in decades.[1]

Osama bin Laden conceded it was 'a great historical event', but did not live long enough to witness the outcome. In fact, the youth-driven activism that powered the Arab Spring revolutions exploded every thesis he held sacred: the divine obligation to wage jihad; Al Qaeda's status as the vanguard; Sunni yearnings for a state built on Islamic lines; and the importance of violence to bring it about. Millions of demonstrators dismissed these theories out of hand, taking as their template the French Revolution, embellishing it with a call for free and fair elections. The distinction between the near and far wars disappeared: Al Qaeda faced intellectual extinction.

After four decades of single-party rule, the collapse of Tunisia's President Zine al-Abidine Ben Ali and President Hosni Mubarak in Egypt exposed an empty political stage crowded with amateurs, few of whom were able to organise an election campaign, let alone a manifesto appealing to the broadest spectrum of first-time voters. Into this vacuum stepped the region's second most enduring, semi-secret organisation after Al Qaeda: the Muslim Brotherhood.

Founded in Egypt in 1928 by Hassan al-Banna, the Brotherhood's supposedly moderate agenda of Islamist revival and practical socialism had gained it wide popularity in the Arab world, while shading its more extreme objectives from non-members' eyes. Beginning in the 1950s, the movement was steadily forced underground in Egypt, Saudi Arabia and other Gulf states.

Nowhere was its suppression more ruthless than in Syria where it had been a militant force of opposition until the Baathist coup of 1963, which brought Hafez al-Assad to power. With its extremist offshoot, the Fighting Vanguard, the Brotherhood was responsible for numerous assassinations of prominent Baathists – including an attempt on Assad himself – which culminated in an uprising in Hama in 1982 that was suppressed with the loss of 20,000–40,000 civilian lives.[2] Membership of the Brotherhood in Syria was punishable by death thereafter.

Grudgingly admired for its work among the poor, the Brotherhood surprised almost everyone when it emerged from the woodwork as the organisation most likely to win after Mubarak's fall. Even the United States, which distrusted the Brotherhood's support for Hamas – the militant Palestinian organisation it founded and Iran now armed – understood the significance of a political movement that combines 'the passion of religion with the power of the ballot box'.[3]

The Brotherhood's transnational network of community leaders, long in the tooth and hardened by jail, was the instrument the tiny kingdom of Qatar selected to harness the enormous human potential released by the Arab Spring. Qatar's ruler, Sheikh Hamad bin Khalifa al-Thani, at 57, was a youngster among Gulf despots, and had used his country's conspicuous wealth to promote a foreign policy that was at distinct odds with the interests of Saudi Arabia, the neighbourhood giant and self-appointed champion of the Sunni weal.

Espousing the same Wahhabism as Saudi Arabia, Qatar sought to demonstrate that this purist strand of Islam could be a force for positive change, as well as violent austerity. In 1996 – a year after he overthrew his father in a coup – Sheikh Hamad up-ended the regional information order by launching Al Jazeera, a free satellite news channel that gave Arabic audiences a ring-side seat on breaking news, including the Palestinian *Intifada*, the invasion of Afghanistan, the Iraqi insurgency and Osama bin Laden's thought for the day.

Produced and edited to industry standards, Al Jazeera's programmes put Moslem audiences at the very heart of events, growing an awareness of news independent of state or CNN guidelines. Al Jazeera taught Arab audiences to think outside the box, laying the paving that led to the Arab revolutions.

However, frequent viewing of Al Jazeera's non-news content also exposed millions to 'Sharia and Life', a weekly show presented by Yousef al-Qaradawi, an Egyptian preacher prominent in the Brotherhood. Berated in the West for endorsing the Holocaust and suicide bombing of Israeli civilians, al-Qaradawi was no less vilified in the Gulf for condemning its autocratic leaders. But Sheikh Hamad liked to have it both ways: before Al Jazeera was allowed to become a 'mouthpiece of the Brotherhood', the movement was forced to shut down its Qatari chapter.[4]

This combination of rolling news and televangelism outraged the Arab League – Jordan, Kuwait, Libya, Morocco, Saudi Arabia and Tunisia all recalled ambassadors for one slight or another[5] – but Sheikh Hamad's hospitality attracted an odd collection of new friends. Qatar had excellent relations with Israel and Iran, despite their mutual loathing, and was an enthusiastic mediator in others' conflicts, including between the United States and the Taliban. Its flare for keeping all options open led to the unusual situation where it hosted the largest US military base in the Middle East – and a coterie of financiers bent on arming the very insurgents the United States was trying to kill.[6]

In 2008, Sheikh Hamad spent $900 million for the purchase of four Boeing C-17 military transports, effectively signalling to the Pentagon he had geopolitical horizons that went far beyond show business. Qatar described the airplanes as props to its international relief operations, and there were domestic considerations as well. The C-17 offered an air bridge when Riyadh closed the land border between them, as often happened, denying Qataris fresh food for months.

But another calculation lay behind the order, notably Saudi Arabia's diminished status as a US ally since 9/11 and the Iraqi invasion, which had extended Shia rule up to its northern border. In signing with Boeing, Qatar was also telling Washington it was available to work on US operations up to 2,800 miles away from Doha, the C-17's utmost range.[7]

The Gulf's aristocrats, with justification, blamed Al Jazeera for the Peasants' Revolt embodied in the Arab Spring, but the credit should be shared with the poverty of North African graduates, the influence of Facebook and Wikileaks cables giving an insider's account of the profligacy of the ruling families.[8] Sheikh Hamad was immune as long as he confined his role to media court jester, but when he sought to transform Al Jazeera's soft power into a Brotherhood empire stretching from Tripoli to Damascus, it eventually cost him the throne.

Al Jazeera flung itself into the Arab Spring as if its professional integrity depended on a successful outcome: narratives of people power radiated from the Tunisian epicentre around the Mediterranean to Sub-Saharan Africa, the Gulf, Iran and Iraq, shaking the grip of rooted autocracies. Yet the coverage was not without bias. The channel was indifferent to people power when exercised by Shia protesters in Bahrain, a state ruled by a Sunni minority, and when Saudi Arabia, UAE and Qatar sent forces in to break it up, Al Jazeera's cameras were nowhere to be seen. Yemen, facing its own upheaval, accused the broadcaster of running 'an operations room to burn the Arab nation'.[9]

As the narrative moved from sit-ins to election rallies, Al Jazeera focused on parties that were transparent Brotherhood vehicles, running on questionable campaign finance after decades in the wilderness. Rached Ghannouchi, head of Tunisia's Ennahda party, had close relations with Qatar – his son-in-law and Tunisia's new foreign minister, Rafik Abdessalem, was once head of research at the Al Jazeera Center for Studies. Other Tunisians considered Qatar's loan of $500 million after Ennahda's victory too cheap a price for becoming a 'vassal of the emirate'.[10]

Egypt was more costly, but then the Arab world's most populous state had richer suitors: Saudi Arabia, Kuwait and the United Arab Emirates all waited in the wings for the democratic tide to turn. Like Ennahda, the Freedom and Justice Party, led by Mohammed Morsi, fielded a Brotherhood manifesto, but was cautious on questions about Sharia, women's rights, alcohol and the bikini, pressing issues in a nation reliant on tourism until the Arab Spring scared its custom away. When Morsi was sworn in as president in April 2012, Qatar poured in $8 billion worth of cash and household gas, pledging $18 billion of investment on Egypt's Mediterranean coast.

Dizzy from winning the 2022 World Cup and chairing the Arab League in the same year, Sheikh Hamad's appetite for adventure was unabated. From arms-length coverage via satellite, Qatar took an unprecedented step into the arena of regime change after popular protests against Libya's Muammar Ghaddafi in early 2011 sank into eight months of civil war. As chair of the Arab League, it led the campaign for a UN-imposed no-fly zone and contributed six Mirage jets to the French-led NATO air campaign that resulted.

On the ground, Qatari C-17s airlifted 20,000 tonnes of arms and equipment to rebels in Benghazi and the Nafusa Hills, providing military training there or in Doha. And when rebels stormed Ghaddafi's citadel at Bab al-Aziziya, Tripoli on 23 August 2011, Qatari Special Forces, jubilant in their midst, hoisted the Emirates' maroon-and-white flag in victory. Al Jazeera filmed it; Qatar paid. When the caretaker National Transitional Council (NTC) ran short of money, Sheikh Hamad stumped up $100 million in cash, using Libyan oil as collateral.[11]

Though the Brotherhood had been banned in Libya for more than half a century, Qatari aid was shared between like-minded commanders selected by Ali al-Sallabi, a Salafist preacher from Benghazi who had resided in Doha for many years. One was Abdel Hakim Belhaj, an Islamist who had fought with the Taliban in Afghanistan until his arrest in Malaysia in 2004, when he was rendered to Libya for extensive torture and imprisonment. Belhaj commanded the Tripoli Military Council after the capital fell to the rebels, making him indispensable to any scheme to restore law and order after the death of Ghaddafi.

'Qatar is weakening Libya,' said a member of the NTC, who requested anonymity. 'In funding the Islamists, they are upsetting the balance of politics and making it difficult for us to move forward. They need to stop their meddling.' But Sheikh Hamad held the view that the inclusion of radical Islam was crucial to the emergence of real democracy in the post-Arab Spring world. 'I believe you will see this extremism transform into civilian life and civil society,' he told Al Jazeera in an interview on 7 September.[12]

Who were Tunisia, Egypt, Libya, or for that matter Syria, to disagree?

7

The Road to Damascus

'O glad tidings for Sham. The Angels of Allah have rested their wings over Sham.'[1]

At first sight, Syria's pageant of freedom looked much like the other protests that flared around the Mediterranean in the spring of 2011, but close up it bore more resemblance to Lebanon's Cedar Revolution in 2005, the first of the 'colour revolutions' to root in Arab soil.

The Cedar movement channelled public rage at the murder of former prime minister Rafik Hariri towards a single objective: ending nearly 30 years of Syrian military occupation. What was forgotten was that Syria's presence for much of that time froze a 15-year sectarian conflict that tore Beirut apart, killed 150,000 people and still lay dormant behind the modern political settlement. Would a popular movement in Syria prise open similar fault lines?[2]

Like Lebanon, Syria was a patchwork of faiths, of which Sunni Muslims were a clear majority, but like Iraq, it had been governed for decades by a privileged minority. In Syria's case, this was the Alawites, who embraced a fusion of Shia Islam and Christianity, and hailed from the Mediterranean enclave of Latakia. The Alawite President Hafez al-Assad and his son, Bashar al-Assad, had promoted an Alawite elite to senior positions in the intelligence apparatus and ruling Baath Party; they comprised 80 per cent of all military officers, but counted for only 12 per cent of the population.

The limits of Arab protest had never been explored in a state run by non-Sunnis, but Syrian membership of the Shia axis of Iran, Lebanon's Hezbollah and now Iraq, its logistical support for Al Qaeda in Iraq, the United States listing as a sponsor of terror and the unresolved conflict with Israel, left it uniquely isolated in the immediate region. The only non-Arab ally to which Syria could turn was Russia, which retained a naval base at Tartous, the last outpost of Soviet maritime ambitions in the 1970s.

The arrest and torture of a group of students on 11 March 2011 for scrawling anti-regime graffiti in Dara'a, a city on the Jordanian border, was the flash point of Syria's pro-democracy movement, but the shooting of 15 demonstrators a week later pointed the direction it would take. Within days, Local Coordination Committees (LCCs) were set up across Syria to organise protests and publicise footage of the regime's reaction via YouTube, Facebook and SMS. Though self-selected, the activists who formed the LCCs reached beyond creed and culture to prioritise the nationalist aspirations of the anti-Assad movement.

In late April Dara'a was under siege by tanks, helicopters and Syrian Special Forces. All utilities to Dara'a were cut, including mobile phone and internet networks. As tanks shelled the Old City, military units went from house to house, detaining 2,000 suspected activists. The bodies of 250 civilians were found at the end of the 10-day operation, as well as 81 officers and soldiers, allegedly shot in the back for refusing to fire.[3]

What happened to those taken into custody was revealed by a forensic photographer, code-named Caesar, who smuggled out 55,000 pictures of 11,000 corpses taken at military hospitals and bases around Damascus between March 2011 and August 2013. The photos, used to obtain death certificates without turning bodies over to families, showed emaciated young men, some eyeless, many bearing ligature and tramline injuries associated with strangulation, beating with metal bars, shackling and other forms of torture. A judicial enquiry financed by Qatar found Caesar to be 'a truthful and credible witness'.[4]

In a move of Machiavellian ingenuity in late May, Assad sowed dragon's teeth among the LCCs with a pardon that released 1,500 convicted Islamist extremists from Sednaya and other political prisons into a turbulent society. If the world didn't believe Syria was fighting an Islamic insurgency, as he insisted to critics he was, then Assad would create one, shattering global moral censure and the revolution's non-violent stance in a single act.

Sednaya prison, like Camp Bucca, was a cruel, brutalising and disciplined academy for veterans of Hama and Syrians returning from the Iraqi jihad. 'When I was detained, I knew four or five or six,' said one ex-detainee, 'I now had brothers in Hama and Homs and Dara'a, and many other places.' Among those released were the radicals Zahran Aloush, Hassan Abboud, Abdul Rahman Suweis and Ahmad Abu Issa al-Sheikh, soon to become leaders of armed Salafist groups in the districts whence they hailed.[5]

As Dara'a licked its wounds, regime forces launched consecutive operations in Hama and Homs, key cities in central Syria. A pattern was soon established that paid no heed to civilian lives or the heritage of Roman, Christian, Ummayad and Abbasid monuments woven into the urban fabric: first, a blockade on exit routes and essential services; followed by intensive shelling of opposition districts; and, finally, a ground offensive supported by a militia, known to Sunnis as *shabiha*, or 'ghosts'.

Regarded as an Alawite militia recruited from the Assad family's criminal sidelines, the Popular Committees – the *shabiha*'s official name – attracted Christians, Ismailis, Druze,

Baath Party members, Palestinians and Sunni tribes from the east, in fact anyone who felt jeopardised by the Sunni resurgence. With Iranian support, the committees were rebuilt as the National Defence Forces (NDF), a trained and paid reserve of 100,000 men that the regime increasingly came to rely on as casualties and defections depleted the conscript army.[6]

While the flight – usually called 'defection' – of senior figures, like Manaf Tlass, a Republican Guard general, Prime Minister Riyad Farid Hijab and numerous others, was a useful marker for predicting the regime's longevity, desertions were never as threatening as the media portrayed. Sunnis made up 60 per cent of the army, but were closely watched for treachery and only deployed among Alawite or NDF units to keep them in line. While this restricted the use of ground forces, to the point where the Kurdish province of Al-Hasakeh and Deir ez-Zour in the east were virtually abandoned, the regime proved remarkably resilient as civil disobedience turned to armed conflict.[7]

Colonel Riad al-Asaad, a co-founder of the first, organised military resistance, claimed that 15,000 men had defected out of a total of 220,000 regime troops, but the White House rated the figure as low as 1,000–3,500. Many fled out of conviction or to safety, not to challenge an army they knew from experience was infinitely better armed. One thousand Syrian officers, who defected to Turkey in the hope of joining a US-backed advance on Damascus, were still watching the war on television in a camp for deserters three years later.[8]

Ethnic cleansing in the coastal province of Latakia to secure a 'rump' Alawite enclave began as early as efforts to stamp out resistance in Dara'a. Sunni villagers fled into Idlib, or across the Turkish border to Hatay. In the course of the operation, nine Syrian soldiers were killed in Baniyas, 40 km south of Latakia – the first sign that protest was morphing into revolt or, more alarmingly, that it had been infiltrated to provoke more extreme reactions.[9]

Any further doubt of the opposition's readiness to fight disappeared in Jisr al-Shughour, in the hills of north-west Idlib. Locals claimed the killing of 15 demonstrators at a previous demonstration persuaded them to carry guns. When snipers shot into a funeral procession from the post office roof on 3 June, mourners besieged the building with 'dynamite barrels', gas cylinders and gunfire, killing eight intelligence officers and forcing the others to surrender. Fighting persisted for two days as residents used looted AK-47s, machine guns and grenade launchers to repel a counter-attack in which 120 soldiers were killed. Jisr al-Shughour marked the beginning of the armed conflict and the end of the revolution's non-violent ethos.[10]

As the pace of killing picked up, the United States, the United Nations, the European Union and their members all urged the regime to negotiate, backed by a variety of sanctions, travel bans, asset freezes and a threat to refer Assad to the International Criminal Court. But President Obama was actively seeking re-election in mid-2011: after winning his first term on a pledge to withdraw from Iraq, his presidency was not secure enough to risk the second by embarking on a new Middle East gamble with American blood and treasure. Ambassador Robert Ford, who visited the Hama protesters in July 2011 and paid a condolence call on the family of a murdered activist, told Syrian opposition figures not to expect US intervention of the kind then underway in Libya. 'This is a Syrian problem', he said, 'and it needs Syrian solutions.'[11]

On the eve of Ramadan, Syrian tanks drew up in a circle around Hama where protests had attracted up to half its 800,000 residents on 29 July 2011. The identical method was used as in the Dara'a: siege, bombardment and clearance by ground forces. After three days of shelling, troops and NDF militia burst through the defenders' barricades to take Assi Square, while snipers picked off the residents as they ran for shelter. One hundred civilians were killed in the first 24 hours, a figure that doubled by 4 August, gaining infamy in the Muslim world as the 'Ramadan Massacre'. 'What are they going to do next?' wondered Louay Hussein, an Alawite activist in Damascus, 'bomb Syrian cities and towns with warplanes?'[12]

Another year would pass before Assad unleashed his 50 attack helicopters, by which time Syrian rebels had collected enough weapons to hold territory and ambush any force seeking to dislodge them. Despite worldwide clamour over civilian losses – only 2,000 had perished by the end of the Hama siege – the regime was a long way from exhausting its military options, which included 3,000 artillery pieces, hundreds of fixed-wing aircraft, ballistic missiles, cluster bombs, chemical weapons and a range of improvised devices, including 'barrel' and chlorine bombs; not to speak of hunger, thirst, trauma, mutilation, rape, destruction, exile and the other side-effects of prolonged siege. All these weapons would be hurled against Syria's civilians over the next five years as 'strict counter-insurgency morphed into collective punishment and verged on wholesale scorched earth policy'.[13]

Not since the break-up of Yugoslavia had siege, and the different methods of besiegement, occupied such prominent roles in the conduct of modern war, but the wasting of Hama, Homs and Aleppo induced the same glazed inertia as had Vukovar, Dubrovnik and Sarajevo 20 years earlier. Accustomed to act in unison, or not at all, governments in the West stood by as the dictatorship embarked on the slow but systematic extermination of its opponents, fully aware that not one would reach out and stop it.

Robert Mood, head of a 300-strong UN mission tasked in April 2012 with the only ceasefire proposal to date, wrote:

My understanding and experience from Syria was that the crisis could have been solved if the international community had offered the president and his government an honourable way forward during the summer of 2012. Saving face and honour were much more important ingredients than life or death for these key individuals [...] In official, as well as unofficial discussions, we experienced their fear of exposing any sign of weakness. Standing up against international pressure was seen as demonstrating self-confidence and strength.[14]

As regime forces closed in on Hama in July, seven defecting officers announced the creation of the Free Syrian Army to 'protect the people from the armoured killing machine of the system'. The LCCs, still coordinating protests inside the besieged cities, objected; they gave Israel's repression of the second Palestinian *Intifada* as an example of what would happen if the revolution resorted to violence.

'Militarisation would put the Revolution in an arena where the regime has a distinct advantage, and would erode the moral superiority that has characterised the Revolution since its beginning'.[15]

8

Prince Bandar's Last Adventure

The creation of the Syrian National Council (SNC) in September 2011, after a conference of the opposition in Istanbul, exposed a rift that would have untold consequences in shaping the armed revolt. Intended as the framework for a transitional government after Assad's fall, the SNC was dominated by Brotherhood exiles, headed by Ghassan Hitto, a US citizen who was elected prime minister in waiting two years later.[1]

Prime Minister Recep Tayyip Erdoğan of Turkey and his Justice and Development Party were indebted to Brotherhood ideology and welcomed its comeback in Tunisia and Egypt. Turkey shared a 400km border with Syria, so was destined to take the lead in coordinating the movement of arms, supplies and personnel to the rebellion. To Saudi Arabia, that looked as if Syria might be wrenched out of the dreaded Shia axis only to participate in a Brotherhood alliance from Turkey to Tunisia – unless the revolution were destroyed.

The CIA set up its Syrian operations room at the US–Turkish airbase of Incirlik in April 2011. Its purpose was to identify candidates for US support among the multiplicity of factions then emerging, using the Free Syrian Army (FSA), the Muslim Brotherhood and Turkey's National Intelligence Organization (MIT) as talent scouts.[2]

In the same month, the future US ambassador to Libya, Chris Stevens, arrived in Benghazi to act as official liaison with the National Transitional Council, seen as the basis of the new post-Ghaddafi government. The embassy had been shut, but the CIA maintained a compound in Benghazi to monitor the dispersal of Ghaddafi's arsenal as his armed forces disintegrated.

Of most concern was the danger that 20,000 shoulder-fired, surface-to-air missiles, or MANPADS, would fall into terrorist hands, because of the threat they posed to military and civil aviation. After David Petraeus was confirmed as CIA director, the United States committed $40 million to a 'buy-back' programme to take the missiles out of circulation.[3] Work between the two CIA offices grew increasingly entwined the more Assad dug in his heels.

Syria had one of the lowest levels of gun ownership in the Middle East, with the result that early rebel operations were confined to areas near the arms bazaars of Iraq, Lebanon and Turkey. But the post office siege in Jisr al-Shughour released hundreds of weapons into rebel hands, turning the Idlib district, near the Turkish border, into the cradle of armed resistance, led by Ahmed Abu Issa al-Sheikh and Hassan Abboud, two inmates from Sednaya. Colonel Riad al-Asaad, an FSA founder, also came from the area.

Al-Sheikh's Sham Falcons Brigade (Suqour al-Sham) was just one of 1,000 rebel groups to form, mostly as self-defence units for a village, valley or a handful of city blocks. Subsisting at first on expatriate donations and top-ups from Incirlik, the most inventive could parlay their pinprick challenges to the regime into an unbroken stream of finance by tapping into the networks of fund-raising 'angels' living in the Gulf, still unconstrained since 9/11.[4]

Despite Sheikh Hamad bin Khalifa al-Thani's enthusiasm for progressive media and the protection provided by the US airbase, he also sheltered up to a dozen AQI financiers, including Abd al-Rahman bin Umayr al-Nuaymi and Khalifa Muhammad Turki al-Subaiy. Diplomatic sources put Qatar's official support to Syrian rebels at $1–3 billion over a two-year period; the unrecorded private donations were hardly a secret from the palace.[5]

Kuwait initially opposed the rebellion, but as the deaths began to mount, Salafist preachers and tribal leaders hosted gala evenings, issuing bank details to donors via Twitter. A sponsor-a-rebel appeal in Ramadan 2013 to 'prepare 12,000 jihadists for the sake of Allah' (at $2,500 per head) raised $350,000 in the first of 28 sessions; a similar event for brigades netted between $840,000 and $3.4 million a year per unit, depending on the number of fighters they claimed. In hindsight, the US Treasury named Kuwait 'the epicentre of fundraising for terrorist groups in Syria'.[6]

Brigades that relied least on aid from the West performed best at the front. They could multiply their forces by paying regular wages, trade arms deliveries for cash and influence, and supply value-for-money feedback to donors with online video updates of attacks. The Kuwaiti preference for groups with Islamist tendencies, like Hassan Abboud's Ahrar al-Sham, however, also skewed what began as a nationalist expression of resistance into a civil conflict with spiralling sectarian overtones. In August 2013 two of Kuwait's brashest fund-raisers, Shafi al-Ajmi and Hajjaj al-Ajmi, congratulated their 250,000 Twitter followers for the hundreds of thousands of euros they had contributed to 'Operation to Liberate the Coast', an offensive in which 190 Alawite villagers, including 57 women, were randomly slaughtered.[7]

One of the 20 armed groups which took part in the operation was Jabhat al-Nusra (JaN), or The Support Front, the organisation formed by Abu Bakr's Syrian envoy, Abu Muhammed al-Julani, by then a US-designated Al Qaeda affiliate. The opening salvo of JaN's campaign against the regime was the bombing of two offices of the General Security Directorate in Damascus in December 2011 – the first suicide attacks in the conflict. At a stroke, they redefined a scattered rural uprising as a fully-blown insurgency along Iraqi lines, capable of organising mass-casualty attacks against targets inside the very walls of the police state.

JaN retained a near monopoly on suicide operations in Syria throughout 2012, thanks to the well-established pipeline of volunteers to the Iraq insurgency. While Abu Bakr would later discount JaN as a mere branch of the ISI, it is more useful to consider its spectacular December breakout as the launch of a fund-raising appeal, in direct competition with Syria's less professional brigades – and wholly independent of its parent body.[8]

*   *   *

The official position of the United States in 2012 was to limit rebel support to non-lethal equipment to improve the chances of a UN ceasefire plan, negotiated by the former secretary general Kofi Annan. Unofficially, President Obama signed a 'finding', or secret order, as early as January authorising the CIA to take all steps necessary to overthrowing Assad, without compromising that White House commitment: in other words, the CIA must not supply arms to the rebels directly, but it might know somebody who could.[9]

On 3 January 2012, two Qatari C-130s landed in Istanbul with the first of the 'cataract of weaponry' Sheikh Hamad would supply across the Syrian border over the next two years. By April, shipments upgraded to C-17s, making 20 further drops by August, each containing 76 tonnes of assault rifles, machine guns, grenade launchers and ammunition. The arms came from Benghazi, where Ghaddafi's arsenal was being scattered to the winds in defiance of the UN ban.[10]

Doha's shipments were distributed through a network of Syrian liaison officers for the brigades, a system fraught with opportunities for corruption and misrepresentation, ideological and military. Recipients were supposedly vetted in advance by Qatari intelligence, Turkey's MIT and their Brotherhood contacts, but the pace of amalgamation between brigades on the ground made absolute accountability impossible.

The Sham Falcons, Farouk Brigade, Grandsons of the Prophet (Ahfad al-Rasoul), Free Men of the Levant (Ahrar al-Sham) and Unity Brigade (Liwa al-Tawhid), strong in Idlib, Homs and Aleppo, received the largest allocations, at the expense of brigades in the west, south and east. A 400 per cent increase in conflict casualties between May and August to more than 6,000 a month proved the arms were having an impact.

A US official complained as early as October 2012 that 'the opposition groups that are receiving most of the lethal aid are exactly the ones we don't want to have it'. To drive the point home, the US designated JaN as an Al Qaeda affiliate in December to compel donors like Qatar to improve accountability in the cross-border weapons stream. While evidence still tends to be anecdotal, rebels and reporters agree that Qatari arms and money were reaching JaN by 2013, though whether directly, privately or through intra-rebel agreements to share Qatari munificence, they could not say.[11]

The CIA felt so exempt from the UN embargo on Libyan arms that it contracted Jeppesen's International Trip Planning Services, a Boeing subsidiary it had used in the 'extraordinary rendition' of suspected terrorists, to arrange flight plans for Qatar's arms shipments, thereby leaving an ownership trail. It was more cautious about supplying the MANPADS, for which the rebels were clamouring: the Benghazi cell was specifically set up to halt the spread of such weapons.[12]

Nevertheless, when authorities stopped the ship *Lutfallah II* in the Lebanese port of Tripoli in April 2012, it contained 400 tonnes of weapons, including surface-to-air missiles, MANPADS and anti-tank guided missiles. That shipment – and a second to the Turkish port of Iskanderun – was deniable because it sailed under a civilian flag but, taken together, they suggested the CIA was less than scrupulous about what was being loaded in the Benghazi docks. The killing of Ambassador Chris Stevens and three others in attacks on the consular and CIA compounds in the city added a further layer of complexity to an already opaque dynamic.[13]

Saudi Arabia was surprisingly circumspect in dealing with the Syrian rebels, given a weakness for any project that undermined Iran's hold on the region. Private donations were banned outside official channels and clerics forbidden from calling for jihad in sermons or social messaging, though nothing stopped Saudis from giving to fund-raising events in Kuwait or Qatar. Riyadh turned down meetings with the SNC, the Syrian government in waiting, because of its domination by the Muslim Brotherhood and Qatar. This aloofness came to an end after 'losing' Egypt to the Brotherhood in the landslide election of January 2012, coinciding with Qatar seizing the initiative in arming the rebels.[14]

To squash Qatari pretensions, King Abdullah brought one of his big beasts out of retirement: Prince Bandar al-Sultan. Ambassador to the United States and a Bush family confidant for over two decades, Prince Bandar had worked on secret US–Saudi operations to arm the Afghan mujahideen and Nicaraguan Contras in the 1980s, and had a healthy contempt for Qatar: 'Nothing but 300 people ... and a TV channel,' he said, 'that doesn't make a country.'[15]

With US backing, Prince Bandar organised a second arms bridge to ramp up operations around Damascus, with Jordan serving as the staging post. Intended to run parallel with the Qatari operation, it also outflanked it by providing Saudi arms and finance to the brigades most likely to control the capital after Assad's defeat. As a precaution, Saudi shipments were distributed through the Supreme Joint Military Command (SMC), created in December 2012 at Western insistence as the unique channel for military aid to 260 vetted FSA brigades.

A new operations centre was created in Amman, staffed by military advisors from the United States, Jordan, the United Kingdom, France and the Gulf states, whose job it was to analyse and approve all SMC operational plans before weapons were released. To the brink of micro-management, according to one commander: 'We all think they want to keep Assad stronger than us, they want to keep a balance – we get enough to keep going, but not to win.'[16]

A mini-arms race developed between Qatar and private donors on the one hand, and Saudi Arabia on the other, with each backing the rebellion's extremist and moderate wings, respectively. Saudi shipments started to arrive in Jordan in December 2012 after a 3,000-tonne stockpile of Yugoslavia-era weapons was located in Croatia, not yet bound by the EU embargo. Between December and February, Saudi and Jordanian cargo aircraft made 66 deliveries to Amman and Ankara, while Qatari flights, exclusively to Turkish destinations, totalled 90 by April 2013.[17]

Saudi support for moderates in the field also coloured its relations with the SNC, the primary channel for relations between the Syrian opposition and its international donors. In November 2012, the SNC was forced to reorganise after US Secretary of State Hillary Clinton lambasted it for being dominated by elderly exiles out of touch with 'those who are on the front lines fighting and dying in Syria today'. Despite changing its name to reflect the inclusion of previously sidelined secular, democratic and minority forces, the new Syrian National Council (SNC) remained firmly under Brotherhood control until a series of seemingly unconnected events presaged the end of its influence – and Qatar's quasi-imperial ambitions.[18]

On 11 June, Sheikh Hamad bin Khalifa al-Thani announced he would abdicate in favour of his fourth son, Prince Tamim, a pious, less impetuous leader. The sheikh had once said he would transfer power in 2016 but, though in good health, the date was brought forward for no specified reason.[19] Three weeks later, Egypt's President Morsi was overthrown in an army coup, the first step in a process that would see his Freedom and Justice Party, and the Muslim Brotherhood in general, labelled terrorist organisations by Egypt, Saudi Arabia and the United Arab Emirates.

Syrian opposition leaders met in Turkey the same week to work out a deal that would satisfy both Qatar and Saudi Arabia. The SNC had elected Ghassan Hitto, the Brotherhood choice, as interim prime minister in March, but such were the divisions within the opposition, he was unable to 'form an administration'. After a second round, the SNC finally selected Ahmad al-Jarba, a tribal leader from eastern Syria with much closer ties to Saudi Arabia than Qatar. 'The Syrian dossier is now in the hands of Saudi Arabia,' said a source in Doha.[20]

9

Knights of the Silencers

A week after US Special Forces killed Osama bin Laden in May 2011, Abu Bakr released a statement advising mujahideen to remain patient and trust in God. It was his first public announcement since becoming *emir* a year earlier, and was written, not recorded, perhaps due to the remoteness of their relations.

Abu Bakr dedicated to bin Laden's memory 100 attacks – 'storming and martyrdom-seeking operations', with 'devices, silencers and snipers' – which he called 'Plan for the Good Harvest'. Among its first victims were 22 Shia travelling across Anbar to pray at the shrine of Sayyida Zainab in southern Damascus. Uniformed men stopped their bus and executed the males, leaving their families to grieve by the road.[1]

More puzzling was whether the ISI was responsible for a car bomb attack in November 2011 that nearly killed Prime Minister Nouri al-Maliki as his motorcade swept through Baghdad's Green Zone. This exclusive district of government, military and diplomatic offices was considered impenetrable, leading to suspicions that the device had been assembled and set by insiders.[2]

Since becoming prime minister in 2006, al-Maliki had exploited the security vacuum to accumulate a concentration of power that bore comparison with Iraq under Saddam Hussein. An alternate chain of command ran from his office to the army's 14 divisional commanders, 11 of them Shia, qualifying it as the 'ultimate Shia militia' in Sunni eyes. Despite the narrowest win at the 2010 elections, parliament had confirmed him as head of the ministries of defence, interior and national security, and the Supreme Court upheld his control of the election commission, the central bank and the main anti-corruption authority.[3]

This unassailable position was reinforced by laws rushed onto the statute books during the emergency, which were never modified for the post-civil-war period. Article 4 of the 2005 Anti-Terrorism Law provided the death penalty for anyone who commits, or assists in the commission of, a terrorist act, and unlimited detention for the wives or relatives judged to have been aware. Al-Maliki's government had detained thousands of Sunnis under Article 4, without charge or trial, but seldom Shia members of death squads. As many as 10,000 Sunnis were still being held under the law in 2013.[4]

Much as Washington desired to wash its hands of Iraq, the security forces were far from ready to tackle the ISI without US support, let alone an external foe. The earliest that that might be possible, according to Lt. Gen. Babakir Zebari, Iraq's most senior commander, was 2020. Tariq Aziz, Saddam Hussein's former foreign minister, said US withdrawal under the Bush timeline would be like 'leaving Iraq to the wolves'. But al-Maliki had made his mind up in December 2010, when he confirmed: 'The last American will leave Iraq. This agreement is not subject to extension, not subject to alteration. It is sealed.' On 21 October 2011, President Obama announced that the last US troops would leave Iraq by the end of the year.[5]

Al-Maliki moved to tear up the truce between the Sunni and Shia before the United States was out of the door. In October 2011, he ordered the re-arrest of up to 1,500 Baathists previously held in US facilities at Camp Bucca, Abu Ghraib and Camp Cropper, detaining them without charge at secret prisons in the Green Zone. On 15 December, tanks and troops surrounded the homes of the two most senior Sunni politicians,

Vice-President Tariq al-Hashemi and Finance Minister Rafi al-Issawi.

Al-Hashemi was allowed to fly to Sulamaniyah to meet Iraqi President Jalal Talabani as intended, but when Iraqi television broadcast his bodyguards' 'confessions' implicating al-Hashemi in the November assassination attempt, he went into permanent exile. Al-Hashemi was charged with 150 counts under Article 4, and sentenced to death *in absentia*. Similar charges were brought against Rafi al-Issawi, but later dropped.[6]

Despite the political upheaval, the tempo of armed violence was still falling, by up to 50 per cent in Ninewa and Mosul. This did not mean the insurgency had ended; but it appeared to be in remission. The ISI was taking $8 million a month from rackets on Mosul businesses, from market stalls to mobile phone companies: Kurdish, Christian, Yazidi and Shia additionally paid *jizya*, the Quranic levy on non-Muslims residing in an Islamic state.[7]

In mid-2012, Abu Bakr announced the beginning of 'Destroying the Walls', a campaign designed to repopulate the organisation's ranks and command by liberating comrades from jail. During its year-long cycle, ISI launched attacks against eight heavily defended prisons, ending with two spectacular assaults at Abu Ghraib and Taji, in which 1,500 to 7,000 hardened militants were set free – depending on Iraqi or ISI claims. Among 47 death-row inmates released in an attack on Tikrit was Abdul-Rahman al-Bilawi, a former infantry captain who was admitted to the ISI's military shura.[8]

Bold in execution, the prison raids garnered a windfall of sympathy from Sunnis who, though they might not share the ISI's vision, wholeheartedly backed strikes against the government's policy of indiscriminate detention, under Article 4.

'Destroying the Walls' showcased two other aspects of ISI's transformation since 2008. The first was the technical ability to organise and supply a daisy-chain of 30 car bombs at sites around the country, timed to detonate on the same day, with a collateral explosion of panic among Shia civilians. Twenty-four such 'waves' punctuated the campaign at 10–14 day intervals.

The second was an adjustment in target selection. 'We remind you of your top priority,' Abu Bakr had told his followers, 'which is to release Muslim prisoners everywhere and [make] the pursuit, chase and killing of their butchers from among the judges, detectives and guards to be top of the list.' Shia civilians continued to be fair game, but the campaign prioritised members of the army and police: the bases, barracks, vehicles and checkpoints where they worked, and the homes where they lived.[9]

The signature tactic was assassination by silenced handgun – qualifying the hit men as 'Knights of the Silencers', like Haji Bakr, Abu Bakr's advisor. Twenty-five *Sahwa* leaders were killed in this fashion during the last six months of 2012.[10] ISI spokesman Abu Muhammed al-Adnani was so pleased with the results that he listed them by province, like the results of a holiday competition.[11]

In December, Prime Minister al-Maliki ordered the arrest of 150 bodyguards and staff working for Finance Minister Rafi al-Issawi, in a re-play of the ousting the previous year of former vice-president Tariq al-Hashemi, since condemned to death. In identical fashion, an alleged confession to terrorism by a security officer formed the basis of similar charges brought against his employer, in this case, al-Issawi. Sunni outrage was instantaneous, but this time it adopted the model created by the Syrian opposition in organising demonstrations against the Assad regime. The Arab Spring had finally arrived in Anbar.[12]

Peace camps sprang up along the Tigris and Euphrates, filling each Friday with tens of thousands of people calling for the removal of al-Maliki and chanting the Arab Spring slogan, 'the people want to bring down the regime'. Beginning in Fallujah and Ramadi, where protesters blocked the highways to Jordan and Syria, protests spread across Anbar, Ninewa and Salahuddin, drawing in supporters from the governorates of Karbala, Diyala, Maysan and Basra where Sunnis are in a minority.

Muqtada al-Sadr, the Shia political and religious leader, fully endorsed the Sunni demands. 'We are with the demonstrators,' he said, 'and parliament must be with them, not against them.' But what the protesters wanted went far beyond what al-Maliki could persuade his Shia constituency to support, even if he were listening: more Sunnis in positions of power; the reintegration of military officers expelled under the De-Baathification decree; the release of all suspects detained without charge under Article 4; and the removal of all Shia security forces from Sunni areas.[13]

Iraqi troops generally responded with restraint to displays of popular opposition, and with due cause. Despite waving Baathist flags and the presence of terrorist suspects, as defined by Article 4, the crowds were law-abiding, threatening only to use violence if attacked. There were many on both sides who wanted just that to happen.[14]

Hawija, a district in the disputed province of Kirkuk, had long been a flashpoint for disputes over land between Arabs and Kurds, and was also a stronghold of Izzat al-Douri's Jaysh Rijal al-Tariq al-Naqshbandi (JRTN). On 19 April, unidentified militants attacked a checkpoint near Hawija peace camp, killing a soldier, before vanishing into the warren of tents. The authorities gave the organisers 24 hours to surrender the suspects, or the camp would be bulldozed. On 23 April, security forces stormed the camp, killing up to 50 people and sparking five days of fighting in which 200 people died.[15]

In July 2013, al-Adnani heralded a car bomb explosion in the central Syrian town of al-Saboura as the birth of 'Soldiers' Harvest', a campaign designed to lead directly to the formation of an Islamic state in two countries. The AQI, ISI – or ISIS, as it now was called – had never ruled this Ismaili enclave north-east of Hama, so singling it out as the symbolic cradle of the new state made little obvious sense.[16]

'Soldiers' Harvest' picked up where 'Destroying the Walls' ended, its name indicating a directional change from releasing imprisoned fighters to the killing and intimidation of members of the security forces. As well as stepping up the number of drive-by shootings and assassinations, ISIS started to rig explosives to the homes of security personnel and demolishing them. At a location near Mosul, it destroyed 22 houses in a single day. But most of the campaign effort was directed at cutting Mosul's road access from Baghdad, in readiness for a final assault on the city at the end of the cycle, the start of the next Ramadan.

By May 2013, the monthly death toll exceeded 1,000 – the worst in over five years. György Busztin, the UN's Special Representative, called on political leaders 'to take an immediate and decisive action to stop the senseless bloodshed and to prevent [those] dark days from returning'. Al-Maliki instead embarked on a course that transformed ISIS into something resembling the militant wing of the Sunni protest movement, a convergence neither expected and the latter certainly did not want.[17]

On 29 December 2013, security forces arrested Fallujah MP, Ahmed al-Alwani, on terrorism charges following a raid on his home in which his brother and five bodyguards were killed. It was the third year in a row al-Maliki had ended by targeting a leading Sunni politician. The arrest triggered clashes across Anbar between army, tribal groups and insurgent forces in loose, but uncharted, combinations.[18]

Five days later, a column of ISIS technicals rolled into Fallujah unopposed by local army and police, burning all Iraqi flags. At an open-air Friday prayers, a masked fighter declared the formation of an Islamic emirate, and a Committee for the Promotion of Virtue and Prevention of Vice to enforce its behavioural code. 'We don't want to hurt you. We don't want to take any of your possessions,' he said. Within a week, the towns of al-Karmah, Hit, Khaldiyah, al-Qaim, parts of Ramadi and Abu Ghraib, and numerous smaller communities had fallen to ISIS.[19]

10

Treasure of Babisqa

A short walk to the south of the border crossing of Bab al-Hawa ('Gate of the Winds') lies Babisqa, a dead city of Byzantium with a ruined church dedicated to the Roman soldier-martyrs, St Sergius and St Bacchus, now the patron saints of same sex unions.

Possession of one or more of the seven official gateways was crucial to a faction's strength because they delivered a stream of income from trucks and trafficking, ready access to safe havens in Turkish refugee camps and, most important of all, a secure passageway for arms and personnel.

Bab al-Hawa was especially prized since it links the oil fields and refineries of Iraq and eastern Syria to Antakya and one of Turkey's largest ports, Iskanderun, 60km away. 'The border posts are like gold,' said one commander. 'If somebody wants to send you weapons and the [Farouq Brigade] control all the border posts, can they do it except under the Farouq's conditions. [...] Does anyone cement their door closed?'[1]

The regime lost control of Bab al-Hawa in July 2012 to a force combining the FSA-affiliated Northern Farouq (NF) Battalion, which ran the diesel and cement rackets in northern Syria, and the Mujahideen Shura Council (MSC), an Aleppo-based group of foreign fighters whose name identified it as sharing al-Zarqawi's structural model. The two groups promptly fell out.[2]

After regime forces withdrew, the MSC filmed its vehicles driving through Bab al-Hawa flying Al Qaeda flags, defying an NF video commitment that Al Qaeda was not welcome in

Syria.[3] After the MSC clip went online, Turkey interrupted arms deliveries for 22 days just when they were most needed in Homs.[4] Led by Firas al-Absi, a Saudi-educated Syrian and professional jihadist, the MSC had a reputation for kidnapping journalists and was suspected of ingratiating itself with Abu Bakr and the ISI: though not yet present, he and Haji Bakr installed themselves 'at their residence on the Turkish borders' the following April.[5]

The incident at Bab al-Hawa sparked a tit-for-tat killing of the kind that al-Julani had scrupulously avoided in his relations with Syrian groups on their own turf. On 31 August 2012, Firas al-Absi was assassinated by a gunman loyal to Thaer al-Waqqas, the NF commander at Bab al-Hawa, who was later killed on the orders of Firas' brother, Amr al-Absi, who assumed command of the MSC and later gravitated towards the IS Shura Council.[6]

With the two commanders dead, custody of Bab al-Hawa was shared between Ahrar al-Sham, JaN's closest Syrian ally, the Army of Islam and the Suqour al-Sham Brigade, but the keys to the treasure of Babisqa stayed with General Salim Idris, head of the Supreme Military Council of the FSA. Hidden amid the early-Christian ruins were ten newly built warehouses, filled with Kalashnikovs, rocket launchers, rocket-propelled grenades and 200 tonnes of ammunition from Saudi Arabia and Qatar, as well as medical kits, satellite communications devices, ready-to-eat meals and over 100 pick-ups supplied by the United States, the United Kingdom and France.[7]

JaN may have obtained some of this booty through Ahrar al-Sham, but it had less need than others of FSA help. The combat efficiency of its units, and their ability to muster suicide bombers to crack the enemy's spirits, often tipped the balance between victory and rout. FSA groups were keen to work alongside its forces, and fighters lined up to join. Even al-Zarqawi's brother-in-law, Abu Julaybib, fought for JaN on the Dera'a front. JaN's record of successes had increased its strength to 6,000–10,000 fighters by the end of 2012, or 9 per cent of the insurgency, compared to 1 per cent when it entered the scene a year earlier.[8]

And when JaN required more weapons, it simply went to where there were plenty: the regime's bases. In October that year, it teamed up with the FSA and another Al Qaeda fellow-traveller, Abu Omar al-Shishani (Omar the Chechen), head of the Army of Emigrants and Helpers (Jaysh al-Muhajireen wal-Ansar) in a night attack on Aleppo's 606 Rocket Brigade, hauling off its arsenal of arms and ammunition, but destroying the Scuds and radar equipment.[9]

The 606 Brigade base was the first of a string of attacks by JaN and its partners over the winter of 2012 that opened the highway from Aleppo to Al Bukamal, gateway to Iraq's Anbar province, causing Abu Bakr no little concern. Superficially, JaN appeared to be moving east to merge forces with its secret Iraqi parent, but in reality it was establishing prior possession of the oil fields in Deir ez-Zour province. Since the collapse of regime control the previous June, these had lapsed into the hands of factions and tribes, who brewed crude in make-shift refineries for sale to local drivers. Syria's eastern sky was black with smoking oil.[10]

On the day in December 2012 the US designated JaN as an Al Qaeda organisation, its local branch in Deir ez-Zour announced it had joined nine other brigades to form another Mujahideen Shura Council, a sign that a move was underway that required improved collaboration. JaN's eastward thrust began in the second week of 2013 with the capture of the Taftanaz airbase, near Idlib, followed by attacks on the security installations around al-Tabqa ('Revolution') Dam at Lake Assad on the Euphrates – a crushing symbolic loss.[11]

Crucial to the capture of al-Tabqa was the lakeside town of Maskana, controlled by Dr Hussein Suleiman, or 'Abu Rayyan', a popular Ahrar al-Sham commander who had taken the Tal Abyad border crossing away from the Northern Farouq in September, abruptly cutting off its supplies of ammunition. Tal Abyad connected Raqqah directly to Urfa, Turkey, providing a much closer gateway to the Syrian city than either Bab al-Hawa or Bab al-Salama.[12]

Raqqah was called the 'hotel' of the revolution because it hosted 500,000 displaced people displaced from Idlib, Aleppo and a countryside still bowed by drought. That a monument of Hafez al-Assad, the president's father, stood undamaged in the main square two years into the conflict testified to the strength of a non-aggression pact between local sheikhs and Assad that allowed him to defend his eastern assets with nothing more valuable than the 17th Army Reserve Division. As rebel forces converged on the city on 3 March, that agreement ended.[13]

By one account, Brigadier General Khaled al-Halabi, head of state security, 'pulled out on the morning of the attack, handing over the city's eastern entrance [...] to the fighters of the Muntasir Billah Brigade and JaN', under an agreement with local sheikhs to minimise the killing. Another referred to 'ferocious battles' between regime forces and Ahrar al-Sham, until local activists negotiated their withdrawal to the 17th Division base a mile away. By 5 March, Raqqah became the first provincial capital in Syria to fall entirely under rebel control.[14]

As was customary, the participating forces shared the spoils. Ahrar al-Sham claimed the Syrian Central Bank, with over $60 million in Syrian pounds, and the running of the bus, electricity and water departments. JaN, equally typically, demurred, leaving its share to Jabhat al-Wahida wal Tahrir al-Islamiyya (Islamic Unity and Liberation Front), a local tribal alliance, whose commander, a Dr Samer, moved into the governor's mansion. JaN confined its activities to *daw'a*, or religious outreach, and providing bread, cooking gas and clothing to the needy at subsidised prices. The NF, despite capturing two regime checkpoints in the assault, got nothing. 'People don't listen to you when you are weak,' said one of its commanders.[15]

When *Time* magazine's Rania Abouzeid reached Raqqah 19 days later, 'the scars of war were faint'. The real surprise, she reported, was that the Islamist rebels had maintained order, protected property and established a Sharia court to hear disputes. 'If civil peace prevails,' said Abu Tayf, an Ahrar al-Sham commander, 'we will be an example for others to follow, but if we fail, people might even turn away from the idea of liberation.' An unusual truce between jihadis, civil society activists and former state employees persisted for two months, but the sharp differences between them kept intruding.[16]

'The militia takeover of the city [...] was supposed to be liberation, and then pull out,' said Omar al-Huwaidi, a prominent activist. 'Unfortunately, that didn't happen. The fighters, when they took control of the city, they took everything.'[17]

And then Abu Bakr dropped his bombshell.

11

Chain of Custody

In March 2013, the Syrian government asked UN Secretary-General Ban Ki-moon to dispatch a team to investigate a suspected chemical weapons attack on the regime-held suburb of Khan al-Assal, 14 km west of Aleppo. State and independent media agreed that 10 civilians and 16 soldiers had died, and that chlorine gas was the probable cause. Åke Sellström, a Swedish expert who led UN investigations in the Gulf War, was appointed chief inspector, but when the UK and France called for him to look into other attacks, the team was denied entry for several months.[1]

The attack on Khan al-Assal in July 2013 followed the fall of Aleppo's Sheikh Suleiman Airbase to JaN and associated groups the previous December, and the loss of a factory near al-Safira that produced chlorine for fertilisers and Syria's programme of chemical weapons. Loss of the airbase had prompted the regime to warn the UN that 'terrorist groups may resort to using chemical weapons against the Syrian people', while pledging it would never 'use chemical weapons under any circumstances, if they exist'.[2]

Syria's chemical arsenal was far from hypothetical – like the Israeli nuclear programme it was built to deter. Since the Yom Kippur War, Syria had created the largest chemical capability in the Middle East, with the help of the Soviet Union, Egypt, North Korea and Iran. Syria's Scientific Studies and Research Centre (CERS) administered 1,000 tonnes of VX nerve agent, mustard gas and hundreds of tonnes of sarin.[3] A defecting CERS chemist said Syria possessed 3,000 bombs that could be filled with sarin and 100 chemical warheads for use with Scud missiles.[4]

International fears about Syria's chemical weapons centred less on their battlefield use or even that Islamist groups might capture them. The more immediate concern was that they would be dispersed and fall out of sight of the surveillance apparatus that ensured they had remained a manageable risk for 40 years. German intelligence had watched in July 2012 as trucks carted away the inventory of a chemical facility near Homs, in all likelihood to prevent rebels from seizing the stockpile.[5]

A month later, President Obama issued the warning that would return to haunt him the following year.

> We have been very clear to the Assad regime, but also to other players on the ground, that a red line for us is we start seeing a whole bunch of chemical weapons moving around or being utilised. That would change my calculus. That would change my equation.[6]

Previous attacks involving sarin were reported in Otaiba and Adra, near Damascus, Sheikh Maksoud, near Aleppo, and Soraqeb, near Idlib, in March and April 2013. Analysts concluded the regime was releasing limited amounts of gas to block specific rebel advances or break stalemates, but not in quantities large enough to warrant international censure. The defector said CERS had mixed sarin with tear gas to hatch a whole set of new symptoms that experts would find harder to identify.[7]

By mid-May 2013, the threat of toxic weapons was so commonplace in Damascus that rebels carried gas masks as a matter of routine. In Jobar, a rebel position near Abbasid

Square, *Le Monde* journalists witnessed gas attacks several days in a row. The paper reported,

> At first, there is only a little sound, a metallic ping, almost a click. […] No odor, no smoke, not even a whistle to indicate the release of a toxic gas. And then the symptoms appear. The men cough violently. Their eyes burn, their pupils shrink, their vision blurs. Soon they experience difficulty breathing, sometimes in the extreme; they begin to lose consciousness.[8]

Le Monde photographer Laurent Van der Stockt tested positive for sarin exposure after he returned to France. Syrian activists had also smuggled out soil and tissue samples on different occasions, but they could not meet the strict chain-of-custody rules constituting evidence, which require no contamination could possibly have occurred between the crime scene and laboratory.[9]

British intelligence cited 14 occasions on which the regime used chemical weapons and found no evidence of rebel access to them, despite the arrest some months before of JaN operatives in Turkey with two kilograms of sarin in their possession.[10] US intelligence said 100–150 Syrians had died from sarin up to the end of March, but regarded the evidence as too flimsy 'to take to the world', being based only on eyewitness testimony, symptoms and social media reports.[11]

Damascenes had lived a relatively peaceful existence until July 2012 when 3,000 FSA-led fighters infiltrated districts close to the heart of old Damascus and occupied suburbs to the west of the main north–south highway, and in the south-east. Regime forces easily repelled them using artillery, helicopter gunships and heavy armour, but not before a crushing blow had been inflicted on its senior leadership.[12]

Three days into Operation Damascus Volcano, as the rebels dubbed the attack, a bomb killed Defence Minister General Daoud Rajha, Hafez Makhlouf, head of intelligence investigations, the former defence minister General Hassan Turkmani and Assef Shawkat, Assad's brother-in-law and deputy defence minister. Shawkat was chief overseer of the pipeline of foreign recruits to AQI's Iraqi operations and a prime mover in the assassination of the former prime minister of Lebanon, Rafik Hariri, in February 2005.[13]

Rebels still infested the suburbs of Adra, Douma, Harasta, Qaboun, Jobar and Barzeh in early 2013, and had freedom of movement in Eastern Ghouta, an area of farms and orchards, not unlike the Baghdad Belts, which served the same purpose for the Syrian opposition that the Belts did for AQI. Fighters transitioned through Eastern Ghouta to the canyons of mortared buildings and a network of tunnels that connected each to each, like trenches in the First World War.[14] Both sides went underground to evade snipers and access loftier ruins from where they could spot enemy movement across the tidal rubble and post sharpshooters to stop it. 'There are two cities,' said a soldier, monitoring surveillance devices via computer seven metres below Jobar. 'There's the virtual one above, and the real one below.'[15]

Western Ghouta had a similar hinterland, but its populated centres, Moadamiya and Darayya, were more vulnerable to attack, being close to Mezzeh Military Airport, a number of missile bases and the 4th Armoured Division, commanded by Maher al-Assad, the president's younger brother. Control of Western Ghouta ensured the delivery of arms and ammunition from across the Lebanese border, 22 miles west, or from Jordan, 65 miles to the south.

After the formation of the SMC in December 2012, Grad missile, man-portable SA-16s and SA-8 air defence systems became more common in rebel arsenals, posing a new threat to regime control of the sky. As the balance of lethality shifted, the regime launched attacks on rebel supply lines, retaking Otaiba, gateway to Eastern Ghouta, and pushing into Jobar, Qaboun and Barzeh, even as it made ready for a *coup de grâce* by bringing in thousands of soldiers from the Golan Heights. The death toll passed 100,000 in July, a 7,000 increase on figures for June.[16]

With exquisite timing, Åke Sellström and the Organisation for the Prohibition of Chemical Weapons (OPCW) team finally registered at the Four Seasons Hotel on 18 August, five months late, but three days before Operation Capital Shield, a counter-offensive aimed at finally crushing the rebellion in Damascus. Sellström still intended to take samples at Khan al-Assal and two other locations to confirm whether chemical weapons had been used, and of what type. But the OPCW was not expected to apportion blame: that was the task of the UN Security Council, split between the United States, the United Kingdom and France, on the one hand, and Russia and China, on the other – each with a power to veto a final decision.

A year and a day after President Obama issued his 'red-line' warning, eight rockets thudded into Zamalka, Eastern Ghouta, at a little after 2 am on 21 August, without causing alarm. As each missile exhaled its poisonous load of 50–60 litres of sarin, the sleeping residents choked as mucus clogged their breathing passages, painting their eye sockets a strange, pallid blue after their bodies expired.

As the morning lengthened, worshippers at Rawda Mosque in Moadamiya listened as a rocket struck a building at the start of the early prayer, the first of seven to hit the Western Ghouta suburb. The rockets were a staple of Syria's Soviet-era arsenal, the 140mm, designed to carry chemical loads of up to 2.2

kilograms.[17] Activists reported further attacks in Jobar, Darayya and eight rebel-held areas in Eastern Ghouta that night.[18]

The internet was inundated with videos of the dead, seemingly uninjured, laid out in lines under solemn white shrouds, but the scale of loss was harder to determine. Citizens' councils in Zamalka and Moadamiya registered 734 and 103 dead, respectively, and Médecins Sans Frontières said its doctors had treated 3,600 people with symptoms of sarin exposure. Yet intelligence estimates varied between France's 281 and 1,429 by the USA, implying a baffling lack of agreement at what would prove to be a defining fork in the conflict.[19] The dead had crossed another red line into the underworld of diplomacy.

After two days more of fighting, the OPCW team was escorted into the target areas on 23 August. The outcome was never really in doubt, given the regime's enormous stockpile, but questions arose about the motive and timing of the attacks. Regime forces had been winning since April and were on the brink of a major inflection in Damascus: what was the point of defying the US president's ultimatum just when a UN team was in the capital at the regime's invitation?

Intercepted communications before the attacks, and reverse mapping of the rockets' flight paths after them, indicated the base of the 155th Brigade in Maher al-Assad's 4th Armoured Division as the origin and likely initiator of the strikes.[20] Maher was an easy scapegoat, but any clarity was quickly overcast by the competing calculi of subject-matter experts, muttering darkly of azimuths.

Investigative journalist Seymour M. Hersh argued that the Ghouta attacks had been a Turkish covert operation aimed at dragging the United States into the conflict over a falsified transgression of Obama's 'red line', but his information was based on a single, unnamed US source.[21] President Vladimir Putin sided with Hersh: 'No one doubts that poison gas was used in Syria. But there is every reason to believe it was not used by the Syrian Army, but by opposition forces to provoke intervention by their powerful foreign patrons, who would be siding with the fundamentalists.'[22]

Popular logic held that death by sarin was less painful than the many other deaths available under Assad, but if a legal nicety dating to the First World War would provoke the United States to intervene, so be it. The Arab League backed air strikes, with Turkey drawing a parallel with NATO's intervention after the massacre of Muslims at Srebrenica.[23] Popular logic in the West was less enthusiastic, having seeing the consequences of air strikes in Afghanistan, Iraq, Libya and North Waziristan. Only 22 per cent of Britons approved of strikes a week after Ghouta, while US support stood at 46 per cent – but only if Britain and France participated.[24]

The White House was considering two scenarios as it waited for the OPCW to report: a two-day attack on less than 50 military targets with Tomahawk missiles launched from the US Mediterranean fleet; and a second, using US, British and French bombers, with a longer list of targets, including civilian infrastructure.[25] Neither translated exactly into regime change, but both would result in the creation of a no-fly zone over Syria that would reduce civilian casualties and tilt the asymmetric war away from the regime. As the threat of air attack drew closer, the lights dimmed in the Republican Guard barracks on Mount Qasioun.[26]

President Obama's second option exploded on 29 August after the House of Commons, still smarting from the chemical weapons dossier used to justify the invasion of Iraq 10 years before, rejected air strikes against Syria by the thinnest of majorities. Two days later, the president announced his intention to ask for Congressional approval, a tactic he knew would fail because of the Republican majority.

On 10 September, Syria announced it had accepted a Russian proposal to place all its chemical weapons under international control to avoid US military action, and Obama asked Congress to delay the vote. Four days later, an agreement was signed that required Syria to provide a full list of its chemical weapons within a week for eventual disposal by the end of June 2014. 'All of this initiative does not interest us,' said General Salim Idris, head of the SMC. 'Russia is a partner with the regime in killing the Syrian people. A crime against humanity has been committed and there is not any mention of accountability.'[27]

Russia's face-saving solution to President Obama's dilemma dealt a blow to Syria's secular opposition from which it never recovered, without imposing any limits on the regime's use of conventional weapons to crush the pro-democracy movement. 'The revolution is dead,' said one FSA commander, 'it was sold'. Assad had bought himself time.[28]

12

Game of Thrones

If JaN's style of jihad seemed to wear flowers in its hair, it was due to Abu Mohammad al-Julani's reading of Abu Musab al-Suri (Mustafa bin Abd al-Qader Setmariam Nassar), a jihadi theorist from Aleppo with Spanish residency, once described as Trotsky to al-Zawahiri's Lenin.

After his arrest in Pakistan in 2005, the CIA transferred him to the Palestine Branch of Syria's military intelligence for more intensive interrogation and safe keeping – an intriguing choice given the regime's continued assistance to the foreign-fighter pipeline to Iraq. Either there or in Sednaya prison, he was reunited with Abu Khalid al-Suri (Mohammed al-Bahaiya). The two men had fought in the Fighting Vanguard at Hama and in 1997 co-founded the Islamic Conflict Studies Bureau in London, which organised some of Osama bin Laden's first interviews.

One contact he made at this time was Al Jazeera's Taysir Allouni, another Syrian with Spanish residency, who interviewed Osama bin Laden before the 9/11 attacks and was the first journalist Abu Mohammad al-Julani was willing to talk to on camera. In 2005, Allouni was sentenced to seven years in prison for carrying $4,000 in cash to Abu Khalid al-Suri, then living in Kabul.[1]

The two Syrians were released in the 2011 amnesty that was designed to radicalise Syria's peaceful protest movement and push it towards overt terrorism. Abu Musab vanished, but Abu Khalid went to Aleppo to form Ahrar al-Sham, with others from the Sednaya intake.[2]

Abu Musab never pledged his allegiance to Al Qaeda, preferring the role of 'a dissident, a critic and an intellectual'. 'We are in a ship that you are burning on false and mistaken grounds,' he wrote to bin Laden after the US invasion of Afghanistan in 2001, accusing him of catching 'the disease of screens, flashes, fans and applause.'[3]

Three years later, he published his corrective, a 1,600-page online tome, *The Global Islamic Resistance Call*, in which he condemned the traditional hierarchy imposed on jihad – specifically referencing Al Qaeda – and argued in favour of a decentralised approach that he termed 'the third generation of jihad'.

He identified 17 lost opportunities in earlier jihads, among them: providing services to people; avoiding extremism; maintaining strong relationships with local communities and other armed groups; and concentrating on fighting the enemy. Al-Julani had practised these principles with success in Syria since January 2012, but did not admit to Abu Musab's direct influence until March 2014.[4]

In July 2013, *The Guardian*'s Ghaith Abdul-Ahad gave a persuasive account of JaN's neo-socialist policies in Shadadi, an energy-rich town in eastern Raqqah. Water, cooking gas and healthcare were free, subsidised loaves delivered daily, and justice 'swift'. His interviewees dismissed the FSA as thieves and praised JaN's sensitivity to tribal dynamics, particularly in regard to the local deposit of natural gas.[5] But the word on everybody's lips that July was *fitna*: dissension, revolt or schism.

On 8 April – a month after the fall of Raqqah – Abu Bakr delivered a 21-minute radio homily on the phenomenology of Islamist group titles, tracing the phases his command had passed through since its origins in Herat to the instant of broadcast. Henceforth, there would be no more talk of JaN or ISI, but only of a united Islamic State of Iraq and al-Sham (ISIS) combining both organisations: JaN had never been an independent actor, but merely a secret branch of the ISI, financed, manned and led in the ISI's interests alone.[6]

It was an astonishing intervention that divided the world of jihad, and questioned every alliance and attack JaN had forged or fought in the previous two years. Each of its partners would now weigh the consequences to its supply chain once donors got wind they had been working with Al Qaeda all along.

Al-Julani's response was respectful and measured. He denied that any prior consultation had taken place, and while admitting to ISI support, alluded to their different perceptions of jihad: 'We learned lessons from our experience there [in Iraq] concerning what is in the secret of the hearts of the believers in the land of al-Sham under the banner of Jabhat al-Nusra.'[7] He ended by reaffirming his allegiance to Al Qaeda and requesting Ayman al-Zawahiri to arbitrate the dispute.[8] Knowing something of the old man's span of attention, he had also gained time. The two groups' media centres fell silent as al-Zawahiri pondered the entrails.

Shadadi's *emir* of gas, three months into the dispute, said,

Yes, in the beginning, the [AQI] did give us weapons and send us their leadership, but now we have become a state. We control massive areas, and they are but a faction. They don't control land in Iraq: they were defeated. We have been sending them weapons and cars to strengthen their spear against the Iraqi rejectionist government, but now they want us to be part of them. I don't understand.[9]

Perhaps the only one who could shed light was @Wikibaghdady: his account of Abu Bakr's schemes resembles a jihadi cartoon of a half-starved Wile E. Coyote in dogged pursuit of Roadrunner. From a 'portable steel box' at his headquarters at ad-Dana, near Bab al-Hawa, Abu Bakr and

Haji Bakr, his advisor, connive to infiltrate spies, assassins, snipers and finally an inquisition of Saudi clerics to block the rising star of global jihad, before concluding: 'it was impossible to kill everybody' who wanted to join al-Julani.[10]

Six weeks later, al-Zawahiri issued his written verdict, later leaked, which dissolved ISIS, but criticised al-Julani for revealing his links to Al Qaeda 'without having our permission or advice'. Abu Musab al-Suri must have choked on the wording. Both leaders must continue under separate national commands, supporting one another with fighters, arms and money, but 'submit a report to the general command of [Al Qaeda] about the progress of work' after a year.[11]

It was Al Qaeda's last grasp at ascendancy, and Abu Bakr rose to meet it. He rejected al-Zawahiri's judgement on legal and theological grounds, saying that if forced to choose between God's command and that of Al Qaeda, he submitted to the first – blocking any further discussion. 'The Islamic State of Iraq and al-Sham shall endure,' he said in a recording, 'so long as we have a vein that pulses and an eye that bats.'[12] Al-Zawahiri appointed Abu Khalid al-Suri – 'the best of men we have known among the mujahideen' – to ensure that his ruling was carried out. It was a death sentence.

'Nusra is now two Nusras,' said a JaN commander. 'One that is pursuing Al Qaeda's agenda of a greater Islamic nation, and another that is Syrian with a national agenda to help us fight Assad. It is disintegrating from within.'[13]

By one estimate, JaN lost 65 per cent of its manpower after the split, partly because ISIS offered fighters up to $200 per month.[14] Saudis, Iraqis, Tunisians, Libyans, Yemenis – often assigned to JaN on Abu Bakr's direct command – were among the first to defect, as were many Syrians fighting with FSA units. Omar the Chechen pledged his allegiance to ISIS out of fear, it was reported, but Salahuddin, his deputy, opposed the choice and defected to JaN with 800 men.[15]

Elsewhere, it was difficult to say where JaN ended and ISIS began. By July 2013, ISIS had returned to Idlib, Aleppo and Latakia, and expanded into Raqqah, Deir ez-Zour, Homs and rural Damascus, but calculated mergers and tactical retreats were more usual than outright battle. Conflict avoidance was more engrained in al-Julani's nature.[16] JaN surrendered its Children's Hospital HQ in Aleppo to Amr al-Absi, now the ISIS *emir* in northern Syria, but moved its operations command to a building down the street. The two groups ran separate media units, but joined forces with the FSA on the final assault against Mannagh air base. In Raqqah itself, JaN and ISIS were 'indistinguishable', but in persistent flux.[17]

The truce ended in mid-September when ISIS captured Azaz, near the Bab al-Salam border crossing, from the FSA's Northern Storm Brigades, and went on briefly to occupy Bab al-Hama. While the Tawhid Brigade tried to mediate over Azaz, it was also negotiating membership of a Saudi-backed, anti-ISIS alliance with JaN, Ahrar al-Sham, Suquor al-Sham, Liwa al-Islam and others, called the Army of Islam.[18]

In Damascus, meanwhile, the use of chemical weapons had lit the fuse that most Syrians prayed would trigger the long-awaited US intervention to end the conflict. When nothing material emerged, the Army of Islam rebranded itself as the Islamic Front. Whatever name it chose, the new alliance further weakened the SMC, already reeling from mass defections to JaN.[19]

Two weeks after the Front was formed, its leading member, Ahrar al-Sham, seized the Babisqa warehouses under cover of night, forcing the guards to flee. The Front called it a pre-emptive operation, at the request of the SMC's Gen. Idris, to prevent the contents falling into hostile hands, possibly ISIS.[20] But an SMC official later said the raid had been a 'complete coup', funded by 'known states', to eliminate the FSA as a functioning concern. The United States and United Kingdom suspended deliveries to Babisqa until further notice. General Idris fled to Turkey after losing Babisqa, and was dismissed in February for being 'ineffectual'.[21]

Serious fighting broke out between Islamic Front/JaN and ISIS in December after the abduction and killing of Abu Rayyan, Ahrar al-Sham's popular commander in Maskana. His body, released two weeks after his death, showed signs of torture, sparking protests across Aleppo and Idlib in which ISIS was accused for the first time of being an 'agent of the state', or *Sahwa*.

It was a provocative, but rational assessment of a group that had committed multiple attacks on rebel commanders and activists since early December, but only rarely turned its guns on the regime's forces. When JaN recaptured ISIS' command centre in Aleppo's Children Hospital – once its own headquarters – it found 50 executed rebel fighters and 300 prisoners, many of them media activists.[22]

Eleven of the wards were used as prison cells; it was there the Western hostages, James Foley, John Cantlie and Matthew Schrier, were held until their transfer to ISIS custody, according to Peter Theo Curtis, who was ransomed, thanks to Abu Marya al-Qahtani, al-Julani's spiritual advisor. He recounted later,

The real issue between the Nusra Front and the Islamic State was that their commanders, former friends from Iraq, were unable to agree on how to share the revenue from the oilfields in eastern Syria that the Nusra Front had conquered.[23]

After six months of recondite study – in which 3,000 fighters and civilians lost their lives – al-Zawahiri published his definitive ruling on 2 February. 'The [ISIS] is not a branch of Al Qaeda,' he declared, 'the latter is not bound by organisational ties to it, and it is not responsible for the [ISIS]'s actions.' For the first time in its history, Al Qaeda had publicly disowned a jihadist group – but it was too late to stop the *fitna*.

Jihadi scholars argued that bin Laden's endorsement of al-Zarqawi's declaration of an Islamic state in Iraq in 2006 had relegated Al Qaeda to the status of a consultative body with no alternative but to submit to God's representative on earth, Abu Bakr, rather than lord it over ISIS as a self-appointed arbiter. Others said that al-Zawahiri's division of the jihad into national branches for Syria and Iraq was equivalent to 'admitting the legitimacy of the Sykes–Picot', the secret Franco-British agreement that re-defined post-Ottoman borders in 1916 and was anathema to those who believed in an indivisible Muslim statehood.[24]

It was a no-win situation, particularly for Abu Khalid al-Suri, whom al-Zawahiri had named his troubleshooter. On 23 February 2014, he died in a suicide-bomb attack in Aleppo that was blamed on ISIS. His murder so rattled the community of global jihad that one theologian compared it to the death of Osama bin Laden. In a eulogy, 'I wish you lamented me', al-Julani accused ISIS of being 'misguided *Sahwa* forces whose goal it is to undermine the jihad' and gave Abu Bakr five days to explain the killing of Abu Khalid to a jury of three clerics – all languishing in prison at the time.

'If you reject God's judgement again,' he warned, '[…] the believers shall fight your ignorant, aggressive thought and, you know, hundreds of virtuous brothers are awaiting a signal from the nation in Iraq.'[25]

13

Paradise Square

Raqqah's freewheeling ride as Syria's first fully liberated city ended abruptly when JaN's *emir*, Abu Saad al-Hadrami, defected to ISIS, a move he regretted when he was overruled by ISIS' provincial governor, Abu Luqman, another Sednaya inmate. Al-Hadrami pulled out, leaving ISIS to share Raqqah with Ahrar al-Sham and the FSA-linked Ahfad al-Rasul Brigade.[1]

On 14 May 2013, Abu Luqman ordered the public execution of three Syrian officers at the city's main gathering place, Paradise Square, ostensibly in revenge for a regime massacre in Latakia, although two were later identified as a dentist and a teacher, simple Alawites from Homs. The execution signalled to the regime's hidden sympathisers that ISIS would brook no resistance. 'And whoever wrongs you,' urged a video, citing the Quran, 'wrong him in a similar way.'[2]

Ninety per cent of Christians had fled at first sight of the takeover, forfeiting homes and businesses; Roula Dayoub, a feisty hospital nurse, became Raqqah's last resident Alawite in the fall. ISIS began to expel Kurds, giving their property to Arab families from as far away as Damascus.[3]

Tensions rose in Ramadan as the arrests of fighters and activists multiplied. Residents replied with nightly protests, one of which triggered a fusillade of rocket-propelled grenades. Into this darkly festering broth came Fr. Paulo Dall'Oglio, a Jesuit priest who founded the Mar Musa monastic community 30 years earlier and had been expelled for his pro-rebel leanings. Dall'Oglio intended to negotiate the release of an abducted television crew, but may have harboured more ambitious objectives. He disappeared.[4]

In August, ISIS sent car bombers into Ahfad al-Rasul's headquarters, killing its senior commander and forcing the group to withdraw. ISIS defended the attack by accusing the Ahfad al-Rasul Brigade of being 'clients of Qatar, France and Saudi Arabia' – like any other FSA unit – but, in other words, *Sahwa*. Abu Saad al-Hadrami attempted a comeback in September, but was abducted and sentenced to die.[5]

ISIS would only win total control of Raqqah the following year, but it was sufficiently relaxed by then to roll out some of the elements of governance it had imposed in the parts of Idlib, Aleppo and Latakia it controlled – with no notable surge in civilian support. After 50 years of Baathist rule, Syrians were not impervious to religion, but matters of faith were considered a private concern, particularly for the young.

The totalitarian framework of ISIS governance was provided by the *Hudud*, a code of 15 'crimes against God', first implemented by the Prophet Muhammed and only valid within a genuine caliphate. The *Hudud* proscribed death for blasphemy, murder, adultery, sodomy, spying and apostasy; amputation for theft and banditry; and flogging for slander or drinking alcohol. ISIS spread the net by jailing smokers and flogging traders who failed to halt business to pray five times a day. *Hudud* punishments had become a weekly occurrence in Paradise Square, by January 2014.

Enforcement of ISIS' extreme Sharia interpretation, a more detailed code that ran hand-in-hand with the *Hudud*, was the responsibility of *al-Hisba*, a religious police force set up 'to promote virtue and prevent vice to dry up sources of evil'. *Al-Hisba* patrolled the city streets up to 10 times a day in vehicles emblazoned with the ISIS logo, registering 470 violations in its first month of operation.

For women under 45, whose dress and mobility came under *al-Hisba*'s fiercest scrutiny, Raqqah became a prison. Initially instructed to wear an *abaya*, covering the entire body except face, feet and hands, they were then ordered to don a veil, then another garment to hide their shape, and finally a double-veil to prevent men looking in their eyes. After yet more revision, they were 'strongly advised' to dress in black, with matching gloves and shoes. Girls of primary-school age wore the *abaya* until their fourth year, when they were forced to take the veil, even in all-female institutions.[6]

ISIS constantly raised the bar on what was required of women to avoid harassment, with the clear intention of driving them out of public life. Any encounter with an unrelated male was forbidden: women could be detained or fined for leaving home without a *mahram*, or male chaperone, a relationship that required official documentation. This presented insuperable obstacles to female professionals, including doctors, nurses, teachers, administrators and students, as well as the women who most needed their services.

ISIS refined its guidance after the fall of Mosul in June 2014 when it 'advised' females 'to shut themselves away in the women's courtyard' and not to leave it unless necessary because 'this was the way of the mothers of the faithful friends of the Prophet'. The only job ISIS did approve of was with *al-Khans'aa*, *al-Hisba*'s female brigade, whose officers divided their time between policing the dress code and procuring brides for ISIS fighters – a sideline that prospered as Raqqah's economy dived.[7]

Most members of *al-Khans'aa* were 'jihadi brides', wives of fighters from Tunisia, Chechnya, Morocco, France and Britain, and they shamelessly exploited their authority. An *al-Khans'aa* notice advised any woman wanting to marry a fighter to wear white under their black veil, and contact would be made. So fearful were families that ISIS would abduct their daughters, they betrothed them as children to local men so as to shield them from more alien harm.[8]

Al-Khans'aa officers had the power to disfigure any woman who crossed them, through use of the 'biter', a device composed of two spiked iron jaws that were clamped around a wrongdoer's chest. 'They told me to choose between the whip and the "biter"', said one woman arrested for 'inappropriate behaviour'. 'I did not know what it was, this "biter", so I chose it, thinking it would be less painful. My femininity was completely destroyed.'[9]

In its other role as guardian of monotheism, *al-Hisba* officers entered the Greek Orthodox church of Our Lady of the Annunciation in September and defaced the icons, before moving on to the Armenian Catholic Church of the Holy Martyrs, where a crucifix was torn down and replaced by the ISIS banner. A video released the same month showed a class of 50 Raqqawi children wearing ISIS headbands, receiving instruction in how to pray and the need for sincerity while doing it.[10]

The only purpose of education, in the ISIS view, was to teach children the Quran, Sharia and the life of the Prophet, to the exclusion of academic or practical subjects, which it denounced as *kafir*, or apostate. In 2014, it closed all schools, pending a purge of the curriculum, denying 670,000 children education. Parents feared that their bored sons would gravitate to the 'cub camps' where ISIS groomed under-16s for future combat through a one-month course in military training.[11]

In December 2013, Holy Martyrs became the headquarters of the ministry of religious outreach, or *da'wa*, a cornerstone of ISIS state-building. Translated as 'invitation' or 'call', *da'wa* campaigns were intended to ingratiate the population through Quranic recitation contests, study sessions and 'fun days' with free food and ice cream – a tactic undermined by the risk of being named *kafir* for refusing.

That accusation – impossible to disprove – was the sword that hung over everyone in Raqqah, but most sharply those with revolutionary backgrounds. Activists, who led the anti-regime protests, fell silent as ISIS rounded up notables, council members and Alawites. By April 2014, ISIS was holding more than 1,000 Syrians in its detention centres around Raqqah. Souad Nawfal, a 40-year-old female teacher, stood in solitary protest against the disappearances in front of ISIS headquarters.

Civil society only truly collapsed after Muhannad Habayibna, a citizen journalist, was murdered four days after publicly criticising ISIS at a meeting it had called on 17 October to present its programme to Raqqah's leading citizens. 'Someone sent me a picture of Muhannad Habayibna right after his murder,' said a friend, Basel Aslan, another activist. 'I was shaking with fear [...] and I felt that the person who had sent it was in the cafe at the same time as I was.'

He fled to Urfa, with 30 others, although it was regime supporters, ironically, who later claimed the killing on Facebook. 'We never had the courage to call their crimes, even though we knew they were behind it,' confessed one former activist. 'Our fear brought even greater fear to the average citizens of the town.'[12]

Determined to atone, 'Abu Ibrahim al-Raqqawi' built a website to keep the world informed of events in his hometown. 'Raqqah Is Being Slaughtered Silently', launched in April 2014, provided a window in words and pictures onto life under ISIS, the only one available aside from the militants' own feeds.[13]

The website went live in late April with the first images of the crucifixion of seven FSA 'spies', allegedly for trying to set bombs. The men had been blindfolded, shot and bound to crosses, but not nailed, indicating the symbol was more telling than authenticity. Recording such scenes was extremely dangerous because ISIS had mounted security cameras in Paradise Square and shrouded *al-Khansaa* agents were among the people who came to watch.[14]

ISIS assumed responsibility for all basic services in January 2014 after it sprang a surprise attack on Ahrar al-Sham, in which 120 fighters were killed. Throughout all these changes in leadership, Damascus continued to provide salaries and telecom services – while conducting regular bombing raids from al-Tabqa airbase – but the technocrats who kept the administration from collapse had all but fled, particularly the Alawites.

ISIS filled the administrative gap with Arab-speaking professionals from Iraq, Saudi Arabia, Tunisia, Jordan and Egypt, while the jihadi Hells Angels who once terrorised the city were metamorphosed into Peace Corps volunteers, smiling as they handed out subsidised loaves to widows and stoically digging for victory.

By April, Raqqah's new rulers could boast of a new-built market, repaired power lines, filled potholes and the Tishrin Dam still in working order, feeding the perception of business as usual – an impression duly circulated in videos to entice Muslims overseas to settle in Abu Bakr's Promised Land. '[ISIS] is not as cruel as the regime was,' conceded a former regime official, working with the new administration. 'If you don't do anything wrong – according to their standards, not ours – they will not bother you.'[15]

Syrian activists told a different story: electricity reduced to four hours a day; water rendered undrinkable through lack of chlorine; rubbish piling in every street; schools closed; doctors scarce; and rising poverty scarcely mitigated by charity soup kitchens. Much of this inventory was due to ISIS' lack of basic technical skills, but the regime's air strikes, joined in September by the United States, Saudi and Emirati air forces, meant it was an inauspicious period to set about creating an enduring Islamic state.[16]

The campaign to win Raqqah's hearts and minds by seamlessly adopting the regime's municipal duties stopped short of any compromise of the *Hudud*. A little before midnight on 18 July 2014, an ISIS vehicle dumped a pile of rocks in Bajaa Gardens and Faddah Ahmad was brought out to be stoned to death for adultery. When a cleric told residents to carry out the sentence, not a single person stepped forward, said Abu Ibrahim al-Raqqawi, forcing foreign jihadis to pound at her until she stopped breathing.

The blood on her body was impossible to see, he said, because of the black clothes she wore.[17]

14

Birth of a Nation

On 3 January 2014 – the same day that ISIS swept into Fallujah – Syria's two largest rebel alliances launched concerted, surprise attacks that expelled ISIS from Idlib, Latakia and Aleppo in less than one week, and reduced its garrison in Raqqah to a single stronghold in the Governor's Palace. It was a rare display of coordination that hinted at the commanding influence of an external actor. With the Geneva II talks weeks away, the time was ripe for a token of the insurgency's ability to keep order in its own backyard.[1]

The offensive was hardly conclusive. Haji Bakr, ISIS' military strategist, was killed in northern Aleppo, but commanders elsewhere negotiated truces that allowed them to pull men and weapons back to less exposed positions closer to their natural centre of gravity astride the Syria–Iraq border, including the temporary capital of Raqqah. A convoy of ISIS reinforcements arrived at this time through Ninewa, the first to cross the frontier heedless of interception.[2]

Deir ez-Zour, Syria's easternmost province, is an oil-rich wasteland that runs along both sides of the Euphrates to the Iraqi border at Al Bukamal, the source of much haulage income – and with close links to the tribal alliances in the next-door province of Anbar. Al Bukamal fell into rebel hands in 2012 when the regime withdrew to improve its chances of holding the cities of the central spine. Since then, each tribe had secured a share of the province's 11 oil fields, creating a new class of warlord: the 'oil thieves'.

Their power derived from selling low-grade crude through Bab al-Hawa and Tal Abyad crossings, at up to $50 per barrel. JaN had created a portfolio of loyalty among the oil thieves, either due to al-Julani's mistaken celebrity as the Syrian responsible for the fighter pipeline to Iraq or his own gift for working with the grain of local revolt, however mismatched in ideology. He may even have been a native: Shuhail, the town rumoured to be his birthplace, was known as Al Nusra City in February 2014.[3]

ISIS reacted to the January attacks with surprising agility, enabling it 'to transition from defence to offence in fewer than 10 days.'[4] Snappy counter-attacks restored Raqqah, where ISIS executed 100 Ahrar al-Sham and JaN prisoners, including Abu Saad al-Hadrami; and extended its territory to the Tal Abyad crossing, formerly controlled by Ahrar al-Sham.

West of the Euphrates, ISIS took Jarablus, Menbij, al-Bab and al-Maskaneh – important choke points on rebel supply lines into Aleppo. In early February, the dramatic repentance of the leader of the dominant Ahrar al-Sham unit yielded Shadadi, in Al-Hasakeh province on the middle Khabur River, opening up a back road into Deir ez-Zour.[5]

The five-day ultimatum al-Julani had given Abu Bakr after the murder of Abu Khaled al-Suri matured on 28 February 2014, a month after al-Zawahiri formally renounced ISIS. JaN was, therefore, at war with ISIS as March beckoned, but it would take another month for hostilities to erupt in Deir ez-Zour. On 30 March, ISIS launched an attack on Markadeh, on the Khabur, in what it called a campaign against the 'Coalition of Jolani and the *Sahwa*[t]', an epithet not lost on the tribes who rallied to JaN to defend their oil investments.

Their alliance withstood an attack on Al Bukamal on 10 April, but ISIS had sent a second force south along the Khabur River to seize Deir ez-Zour from the rear; this met with little resistance until it reached as-Suwar, where ISIS and JaN both suffered heavy losses. A third column, meanwhile, was speeding in from Raqqah with the goal of joining the southbound force at the ISIS command post in Jadid Ekaydat, 10km from where the Euphrates and Khabur converge at al-Basira.

On 26 April, 1,500 Syrian rebels pressed a new attack on Raqqah, which failed but had the effect of temporarily disrupting the ISIS advance on Deir ez-Zour. On 2 May, al-Zawahiri made a final appeal for a halt to the fighting, without success. By early June, the Deir ez-Zour campaign was estimated to have killed over 600 fighters and driven 130,000 people from their homes.[6]

Following another series of defections and broken truces, JaN, Ahrar al-Sham and their tribal allies surrendered their positions in Deir ez-Zour on 14 July, leaving ISIS in control of 95 per cent of the province, but only half of its capital. The northern half of Deir ez-Zour city and the airport were still occupied by Syrian army units, which had watched in amusement as the rebels tore one other to pieces.[7]

They were in a very different mood in September when, wreathed in victory, ISIS finally turned its attention to them.

* * *

The tribal authorities in Ramadi and Fallujah reacted differently to the ISIS takeover, either through fear of reprisal for their activities as *Sahwa*, or varying calculations as to how the parliamentary elections in April might reshape the political impasse. Ahmed Abu Risha, who had spearheaded the Sunni protest movement in Ramadi, now committed his fighters to a government offensive that killed 60 ISIS fighters before ridding the city of militants.[8]

Elsewhere in Anbar, some clans merged with ISIS, while others resisted both militants and the Iraqi army to defend a moderate Sunni solidarity that neither seemed willing to countenance. Fallujah lay somewhere in between. Memories of the US siege a decade earlier and AQI's brutal occupation in 2005–06 were still fresh. Fallujans had no desire to relive these events, but reconciliation with the government was unthinkable after the battering the Sunni had taken in the three years since the United States withdrew. The Military Council of Tribal Revolutionaries of Fallujah (MCTRF), a self-defence force that blended all shades of Fallujan ideology, persuaded ISIS to transfer its forces to the city's outskirts, but this failed to satisfy Nouri al-Maliki, who insisted that Fallujah expel the militants, or face bombardment.[9]

'This is a fight that belongs to the Iraqis,' said Secretary of State John F. Kerry, echoing the US ambassador's advice to Syria's opposition three years earlier. 'We are not, obviously, contemplating returning. We are not contemplating putting boots on the ground. This is their fight, but we're going to help them in their fight.' By the end of January, the Obama administration had approved a $6.2 billion sale of Apache helicopters, drones and Hellfire missiles to Iraq, despite Congressional fears that al-Maliki would use them against the Sunni.[10]

Taking a leaf from Assad's siege manual, the government cut electricity to Fallujah in late January and began an indiscriminate shelling by land and air. The International Committee for the Red Cross, the only organisation allowed access after a ban on media, reported closed schools, acute shortages of food, medicines and milk formula, and hospitals swamped with casualties. By mid-March, 300,000 people had fled the fighting.[11]

Al-Maliki's promise of a ground assault had still not materialised by May when Iraqi journalists reported that barrel bombs had been dropped on Fallujah's 'mosques, houses and markets': in a Syrian context, this usually meant soldiers were too disheartened to advance into an urban battlefield haunted by snipers and suicide bombers. As many as 6,000 Iraqi troops had reportedly died in the four-month operation – but double that number had deserted.[12]

The capture of Fallujah Dam in late January 2014 introduced another weapon into the equation: water. In a bid to disrupt the government attack on Fallujah, ISIS closed the dam's 10 gates, causing widespread flooding upstream and the displacement of 50,000 people between Fallujah and Abu Ghraib. When the rising water level began to threaten its own positions, ISIS re-opened the gates, releasing a wall of water that swamped farmland 160km to the south and sharply reduced supplies of drinking water to Karbala, Najaf and Babil.[13]

The rapid expansion of ISIS' Iraqi lands in 2014 seems predicated on a surge in fighting numbers best explained as the result of mergers with existing militant groups or *Sahwa* units, yet there is no evidence whatsoever to support the argument. In Fallujah, ISIS appropriated the MCTRF's decision to stand firm, absorbing it into the general narrative of Islamic statehood, but this was because its commander chose not to apply ISIS' more exacting tariffs of allegiance and mass executions of hostages, reducing the possibility of fratricide. It was a gamble that paid off as al-Maliki's vindictive reaction transformed Fallujah into a Sunni Stalingrad and a beacon of Shia repression visible around the world.

But there is no evidence that the tribes subscribed to ISIS' grand design before it conquered northern Iraq in June, and more, in the form of grisly massacres, that illustrate quite how resilient the opposition was in Anbar even as the Iraqi state headed for collapse. Iraq's main insurgent groups had always clashed with the ISI over its high-flown demands for submission to Abu Bakr and the Islamic lifestyle; even the conservative Jaysh Rijal al-Tariq al-Naqshbandi (JRTN), seemingly such a close fit with the ex-Baathists running ISIS, was as likely to fight against it, as for it.

In the run-up to the April elections, the assassination of a JRTN commander by ISIS in Diyala triggered a faction fight that killed 70 fighters from both sides and other attacks, over primacy of command or spoils, occurred in Salahuddin, Kirkuk and Ninewa – even as ISIS and JTRN were reportedly colluding on plans to capture Mosul.[14]

An attack had been expected since late May, but Mosul's defences were compromised by a late order to send troops and armour to Samarra where ISIS mounted a diversionary raid the day before its assault on Iraq's second biggest city. Instead of 25,000 soldiers and police, less than 10,000 men were at their posts, desperately short of weapons and ammunition, according to Lt. Gen. Mahdi Gharawi, who was later charged with dereliction of duty for his role in Iraq's most humiliating defeat since the US invasion.

At 2.30am on 6 June 2014, a convoy of pick-ups, mounted with machine guns and each carrying four fighters, raced in across the Syrian desert, shooting past the lightly-manned checkpoints, and into the Sunni districts of western Mosul where sleeper cells were already stirring. The vehicles fanned out to attack and then capture the provincial administration block, two television channels, numerous police stations, the central bank and the military airport, where billions of dollars of US-supplied weaponry was stockpiled: Abrams tanks, medium artillery, howitzers, Humvees, MANPADS and Chinese anti-tank missiles.[15]

The fighting for western Mosul raged for three days. Gharawi said there were insufficient soldiers to mount a counter-attack but, even in their reduced state, they still outnumbered ISIS by more than 15 to one. Al-Maliki spurned two offers by Kurdish President Massoud Barzani to send *peshmerga* to bolster the defences, while the 2nd Division, unscathed on the east bank, was more alert to the threat of a Kurdish incursion than the gains ISIS was making across the Tigris to the west.

A belated effort to mobilise the 2nd Division may have triggered the panic that swept through the Iraqi forces on the evening of 9 June. Two more senior generals, whom al-Maliki personally selected, crossed the Tigris in convoy to establish a new command post in the east, but the manoeuvre gave rank and file the impression they were being abandoned. 'This was the straw that broke the camel's back,' said Gharawi. Within hours, most of the 2nd Division had deserted, shedding their uniforms as they fled in tracksuits and sandals to the Shia south.

ISIS pursued them as far as Tikrit, Saddam Hussein's home town and the site of what would become known as the 'largest sectarian atrocity in Iraq's recent history'. On 12 June 2014 the US-trained officers at Tikrit Air Academy, formerly Camp Speicher, ordered their 3,000 cadets to hand over weapons and board military trucks waiting on the highway for evacuation to Baghdad.

When the trucks failed to appear, the cadets started walking until they reached Tikrit University where 100 ISIS fighters were waiting in armoured vehicles. Photos posted on social media showed the fighters forcing the captives into shallow trenches near Tikrit's Water Palace, where gunmen sprayed them with bullets. As many as 1,700 Shia servicemen were killed that day, and the mass graves are still being located.[16]

Meanwhile, in Mosul, ISIS fighters had divided the 3,000 inmates of Badoush Prison into two groups, herding non-Sunnis onto trucks that were driven into the desert. Six hundred Shia and several dozen Christians were ordered to form a line at the edge of a ravine where they were each executed with a bullet in the head. The fighters then set fire to the bushes around the ravine and the flames spread to the corpses.[17]

15

Twitter Caliphate

The killing of journalist Marie Colvin in February 2012 in what her photographer Paul Conway, an ex-artilleryman, called a 'bracketed' set of rockets aimed at nailing their position in Homs was the first step towards the end of independent reporting from Syria, but not the most important. Journalists continued to defy the regime's restrictions on access as long as they could count on their rebel hosts for frontline protection, and during the most perilous phases of entry and exit.

That trust began to dissolve in 2012 as northern Syria fragmented into a motley collection of factional tenancies, shared between native rebels and privately-funded Salafi groups, swollen by cocksure immigrant fighters. The latter branded anyone claiming to be a journalist as a hostile witness or the agent of a foreign intelligence service.

The physical danger increased as Syrians came to realise that the media were superfluous to any curb on their suffering, and withdrew their permissive hospitality. 'At first they said they thought the world didn't know,' said journalist Rania Abouzeid. 'With time they came to believe that it knew, it just didn't care.'[1]

In July 2012, two photojournalists, John Cantlie and Jeroen Oerlemans, had strayed into a reception camp for foreign fighters near Bab al-Hama, mainly north British or London youths. They were handcuffed, blindfolded, kicked and called 'Christian filth', while 'a knife was sharpened to behead them'. A week later, the FSA rescued the photographers, now recovering from gunshot wounds, before they could be transferred to an 'Al Qaeda-affiliated group'. 'The longer this goes on,' said Cantlie, 'the nastier it will get for all of us.'[2]

The abduction in August 2012 of Austin Tice, a freelance journalist and former US marine, was the first of numerous kidnappings that convinced most Western reporters to stop going into Syria by the end of 2013. Regime or rebel, his abductors made no further request for ransom and, after a 47-second video released two months later, Tice was never seen again.

This method of kidnapping, without comment, demand or even a corpse, was more typical of Latin America than Al Qaeda, and it established a pattern until October 2013, by when 16 journalists had gone missing, including – for a second time – John Cantlie, who was travelling this time with the US photographer, James Foley, and Steven Sotloff, another American journalist. 'The sheikh who originally captured James Foley and me in November 2012,' wrote Cantlie later, 'said: "To go through this, you will need a heart of stone".'[3]

An internet jihadi forum in September 2013 had advised 'capturing every journalist, identifying the equipment they use to report the news, and body-search them for chips'. C. J. Chivers of the *New York Times*, Paul Wood of the BBC and *Newsweek*'s Janine di Giovanni suspended field visits. 'I can take anything but kidnapping,' said di Giovanni.[4] Aid workers were equally vulnerable: the UK's David Haines was taken in Atmeh where he worked at the Olive Tree displaced camp; Alan Henning, while he travelled in a relief convoy; and the American, Peter Kassig, on an aid mission to Deir ez-Zour.

All these men – female journalists seemed exempt because of gender, or the more roadworthy disguise of a *abaya* – were confined in ISIS prisons for up to 20 months with no word escaping outside. Like the regime it claimed to be fighting, ISIS targeted any free agent from reporting, yet vaunted its own atrocities with all the aplomb of a totalitarian regime, but more heedless of exposure.

Since July 2013, ISIS had abducted, tortured and executed scores of Syrian journalists and activists, without attracting widespread attention, yet it paused before inflicting the same treatment on its international trophies. Why? One possibility is that ISIS simply did not know how to make use of them until mid-2014 when it unveiled, seemingly out of mid-air, a structured campaign of psychological operations in print, video and social media, which coincided with its most spectacular military conquests and gave the fullest expression of how the Islamic state perceived its mission.[5]

In fact, the ingredients of ISIS visual propaganda had not much altered since the Destroying the Walls campaign in 2012, when Al Furqan, the ISI's chief media arm, released a 50-minute, high-definition video of a complex attack it had conducted in Anbar. Beyond the signature execution of Iraqi police officers with silenced pistols to the head, the camera collects vanity-shots of ISI's growing professionalism: fleets of pickups, live-fire training, body armour, night-vision goggles, and footage of raids on checkpoints. This video, and others that followed in 2013, were primarily operational diaries, intended to impress and frighten, but not to engage or recruit.[6]

Some of the most vivid transformations to occur over the next 20 months are of subject matter, resource availability and channels of distribution. But most striking of all is the compelling sense of a new intelligence behind ISIS' psychological operations: not a ruthless mastermind, more a rounded professional able to marry specific strands of output to different marketing needs, build them into a holistic strategy, and do it ahead of deadline: specifically the week of 29 June 2014, which marked the start of Ramadan, the fall of Mosul, the declaration of the Islamic State and the symbolic destruction of the Sykes–Picot border between Iraq and Syria.

This individual – or group – had a fluent understanding of social media potential and a kindred sense of the tastes of the ISIS core audience, suggesting the involvement of convert consultants from the Indian subcontinent or perhaps one of the more Twitter-literate Gulf sheikdoms. Two key events in ISIS' media relaunch occurred in April 2014: the creation of ISIS' multilingual Al-Hayat Media Center, soon to rival Al Furqan as a distributor of ISIS videos, as well as their executive producer; and the release of Dawn of Glad Tidings, an Arabic-language app that connected ISIS to its followers, and provides a stream of centrally audited updates, videos, images and tweets.[7]

Al-Hayat's primary service was the production of English-language videos to boost recruitment of fighters and fellow-travellers in the UK, North America, Australasia and the broader English-speaking world. Its first production, *Sound of Swords Clashing 4*, was a feature-length saga with executions, bombings and scenes of carnage, also shot in high definition, but distinguished from Al Furqan's output by the quality of its graphics and use of corporate logos.

Its second, *There is No Life Without Jihad*, released on 19 June, received widespread attention because it showed the first interviews with fighters from Wales and Scotland, and touched on one reason why alienated foreign youth were attracted to the ISIS struggle. Circulated a week after the Iraqi army's breathtaking capitulation at Mosul, the 13-minute video addresses the mental well-being that results from self-sacrifice. 'When I used to live there, in the heart you feel depressed,' said Brother Abu Bara' al-Hindi, from Aberdeen. 'The cure for the depression is jihad.'[8]

Al-Hayat went into a frenzy of activity after the caliphate was first declared, releasing 11 videos in July that urged foreign

Muslims to fulfil their religious duty by emigrating to the Islamic state. For recruits needing more formal persuasion, the media centre had mapped out a full-colour magazine, *Dabiq*, named after a Syrian village where Muslim and Christian armies are predicted to clash in an ultimate battle before the world ends.

'Do not worry about money or accommodations for yourself and your family,' reassured the third issue, in written confirmation of the caliph's promise a month before. 'There are plenty of homes and resources to cover you and your family.'[9]

Dabiq coordinated on a monthly basis with IS' contemporary military or propaganda campaigns, providing a surface legitimacy to such practices as sex slavery, concubinage, mass slaughter and crucifixion, through citations from the Quran and Islamic history, all expressed in a curiously solicitous tone. The 64-page format allowed Abu Bakr's more feverish revelations to be portrayed with a density of detailed sanctimony impossible in video or tweets – though they might be ignored without the latter's fervent cross-marketing.

Even as it seeks to describe the future, however, *Dabiq* is trying to invent a past: one in which Al Qaeda never rejected ISIS; AQI had always intended to destroy the Sykes–Picot borders; and the utterances of Abu Musab al-Zarqawi are venerated as scripture.

The craft and cash lavished on Al-Hayat's videos, and their exponentially grisly content, are unique in the catalogue of jihadi propaganda. Few cast in ISIS' horrific videos survived the experience, but two, like Scheherazade, went on to repeat the previous night's performance: a sign that the producers, initially sated by the glamour of violence, had suddenly discovered the advantages of character development.

One of these performers – the executioner – increasingly became the captive of stereotype; the other – the hostage – was liberated on screen from his orange jumpsuit to an ISIS parody of the job he was doing when he fell into its clutches. 'Jihadi John', as the press called Mohammed Emwazi, the Kuwaiti Londoner who volunteered to behead James Foley, Steven Sotloff, David Haines, Alan Henning, Peter Kassig, Haruna Yukawa, Kenji Goto and unnumbered Syrians, was made to embody the average Western recruit: masked, unformed, discultured and murderous. The photographer John Cantlie, by contrast, grew into the role of reasoning advocate of the Islamic state's authenticity in a series of eight, professionally filmed mini-documentaries that took him from solitary confinement to the frontlines of Kobane, Mosul and Aleppo, but always existentially alone.[10]

Aside from their propaganda value, the films share the singular irony that they are precisely the kind of works that Cantlie may have wanted to present in his professional career, though with less hideous, editorial oversight. He wrote about the production process at length in *Dabiq*.

One observation is that the videos are scripted, and that perhaps I have no choice in the content. This is not true. The mujahideen suggest initial titles, I write the scripts, hand them over for any copy changes that need to be made and the videos are shot. It's all very fast – the first eight videos were written, approved and filmed in just 12 days – but the mujahideen are like that. In quick, get the job done, move on to the next task.[11]

He continues,

I was used to working for the news before, not being the news, and it's very different. Every word you say is examined, especially if you're in my situation. So to really understand the content of the films, and why I say what I sometimes say, you need to appreciate the story behind the scenes.[12]

But it was how IS used Twitter to publicise its activities and beliefs that confirmed it was receiving professional advice on how to access a wider audience. In the same way the internet freed AQI from relying on Al Jazeera and other mainstream media to amplify its messages, social media like Twitter allowed individuals to bypass the online forums that had traditionally moderated debate between jihadis on doctrinal lines. One disadvantage was the loss of ideological control, but it was more than offset by the surge in outreach that occurs when any medium is liberated from the formalities of editing.

Twitter was the most popular application because users could post texts, images and links without 3G or WiFi, and effortlessly retweet – or forward – them to followers. One study of the activity of 59 ISIS foreign fighters gives a sense of the medium's awful power: from January to March 2014, these accounts together generated 154,120 tweets, posting on average 85 images and 91 videos each, to a total network of 29,000 followers – each with the option of retweeting more widely. Though noted for its spontaneity, the researchers concluded from the pattern of content that it was a stream of 'controlled communications'.[13]

In the Dawn of Glad Tidings app, launched in April 2014 to give subscribers instant access to its updates, ISIS found a weapon that could be used to mob its enemies into submission. Prior to sign-up, a user provided enough personal data to covert his – or her – private account into a subject domain which ISIS could use to multiply its transmissions, creating an echo-chamber effect that sounded very like applause and acclamation.

When the Mosul offensive began, Dawn of Glad Tidings generated 40,000 tweets in one day – though the proportion of manual to automatic is not clear – and, as ISIS moved on the capital, thousands of tweets were transmitted with a picture of a fighter, and the text: 'We are coming, Baghdad'. Later that month, IS hacked into millions of World Cup Twitter searches, offering a fans a choice between *There is No Life Without Jihad*, or news of a change in kick-off time.[14]

Arguably, this tactic had less impact on Baghdad morale than it did on mainstream media, obliged by the threat of kidnap to replace on-the-ground reports with social media streams. Nor was this degree of psychological threat especially difficult to orchestrate, according to a study later that year: of 46,000 Twitter accounts run by IS in December 2014, a core group of 500–2,000 accounts, each sending 50 tweets a day, was sufficient to trigger similar avalanches of support. It rattled the Iraqi government enough that it blocked Twitter, Facebook, Skype, YouTube and any data transfer by mobile phone for three days.[15]

Prior to the fall of Mosul in June, ISIS's foreign tweeters sent a series of messages, matey or solemn, evenly weighted between battles lived through, existential questions addressed, with a trickle of everyday scenes and 'selfies': a French boy with an AK47 in a shop, for example, holding that elusive jar of Nutella. The feed started to darken in April as shots of the first crucifixions, taken by the founder of the 'Raqqah is Being Slaughtered', came online, enthusiastically retweeted by an English ISIS account: 'lol become a new false Jesus'.

16
Call of Duty

'I was chosen to lead you,' the newly anointed Caliph Ibrahim told Friday worshippers in Mosul's Great Mosque al-Nuri, 'while I am not the best among you and no better than you.' The hesitant way the black-robed man mounted the pulpit, and his flickering eyeballs, hinted at past combat injuries, but his voice was steady as he related how, in the heat of victory, the mujahedin 'rushed to declare the caliphate and the inauguration of the [caliph]'.[1]

In truth, there was no haste at all: every move since al-Zarqawi announced the Islamic State of Iraq (ISI) in October 2006 had been directed towards this tableau, or one like it, in a different city, perhaps with another cowled figure demanding total obedience in Allah's name. All that was missing was the acreage on which to found this elusive utopia.

Pockets of Diyala, Anbar, Ninewa, the suburbs of Baghdad – even parts of Camp Bucca – had at one time all been annexed to an archipelago subject to ISI's diktat, but the shimmering outline of an Islamic state only solidified after the conquest of Raqqah, Deir ez-Zour and Mosul, like the floor plan of a city uncovered by archaeologists. With the collapse of the Iraq army at Mosul, ISIS suddenly acquired authority over 6 million people along the Tigris and Euphrates, and a domain contiguous with Syria, Jordan and Saudi Arabia that ran as far north-west as the Turkish border.

A week after the Mosul debacle, ISIS sent a crew to film the bulldozing of the man-made embankment that separated Syria and Iraq at Yaroubiya. The gesture was a graphic display of the psychological frailty of the borders demarcated under the Sykes–Picot agreement in the declining years of the Ottoman empire, and a naked threat to the integrity of Jordan and Saudi Arabia.[2]

However, this people of the imagined state were hurrying away as fast as it was being assembled. Within two days of Mosul falling, 500,000 non-Sunnis had escaped to Iraqi Kurdistan where they were joined in December by 2 million refugees from Anbar, Diyala and Salahuddin, other provinces in the fast-expanding caliphate.[3]

Abu Bakr's appearance in the Great Mosque on 4 July was his first in public since Camp Bucca nearly a decade earlier – and his last while alive. Like his predecessor, Abu Omar al-Baghdadi, 'caliph' of the ISI archipelago, he found the limelight distasteful; though whether for reasons of security, to enhance his mystique through rarity, or because, at bottom, he was a man without real authority, is harder to fathom.

His media exposure had been limited to milestones – religious festivals, campaign launches or eulogies – and always by radio. Even on this most solemn of occasions, he spoke for just 15 minutes, while delegating the task of exposition to Abu Muhammad al-Adnani, the official ISIS spokesman.[4]

A Syrian exception within the core of Iraqi leadership, al-Adnani portrayed himself as the ideal warrior-scholar, tempered through years of fighting and prayer. He was six years in Camp Bucca, the last AQI fighter to quit Fallujah and currently commanded ISIS operations in Syria. With the killing of Haji Bakr, Abu Bakr's right-hand man, in January 2014 and Abdulrahman al-Bilawi in the battle for Mosul, al-Adnani's star was in the ascendant.[5]

Five days before the caliph revealed himself, al-Adnani told listeners what to expect in a speech circulated in Arabic, English, Russian, German and French via Twitter. Certain basic requirements, doctrinal and bureaucratic, must be met before a caliphate can be declared: al-Adnani set out to prove that they had in a 35-minute discourse that made the most of his rhetorical skills – while still managing to sound like an exercise in prophetic box-ticking.

Territory: 'The flag of the Islamic State [...] covers land from Aleppo to Diyala'; Defensibility: 'The walls of the tyrants have been demolished, their flags are fallen and their borders have been destroyed'; Religious conformity: 'The Sunnis are masters [...] the unbelievers (*kuffar*) [...] are disgraced'; Justice: 'Koranic punishments (*hudud*) are implemented [...] Governors and judges have been appointed'; Fiscal sustainability: '*Jizya* (poll tax on non-Muslims) [...] *Fay'a* (enemy spoils) [...] and *zakat* (alms) [...] have been collected'; Security: 'The people in the lands of the State [...] feel safe regarding their lives and wealth [...] Evil has been removed.'[6]

There was a measure of truth to most of these claims, particularly in Raqqah, which ISIS had administered for months as a field-trial in Islamic governance and law enforcement to the letter; however, given freedom to voice an opinion, most Raqqawi would say that 'the evil' had been intensified, not eliminated.

Al-Adnani continued,

There only remained one matter, a collective obligation that the Muslim community (*ummah*) sins by abandoning. It is a dream that lives in the depths of every Muslim believer ... a hope that flutters in the heart of every monotheistic mujahid. It is the *khilafa* (caliphate) ... the abandoned obligation of the era.[7]

To avoid the commission of a collective sin, the 'shura council' had appointed Abu Bakr al-Baghdadi as caliph for all Muslims:

'the sheikh, the mujahid, the scholar who practises what he preaches, the worshipper, the leader, the warrior, the reviver, descendant from the family of the Prophet, the slave of Allah.'

The name 'Islamic State' (IS), al-Adnani said, would henceforth replace 'ISIS' in all media communications, and any group, state or organisation became 'null' as soon as the caliphate's forces entered their territory. The pitch rose an octave as the Syrian spoke directly to the fighters.

> We spilled rivers of our blood to water the seeds of the caliphate, laid its foundation with our skulls, and built its towers over our corpses. We were patient for years in the face of being killed, imprisoned, having our bones broken and our limbs severed. We drank all sorts of bitterness, dreaming of this day. Would we delay it for even a moment after having reached it?[8]

Al-Adnani's grandiloquence split listeners between those who genuinely aspired to a caliphate, even if it fell short of perfect legitimacy, and those who considered it a species of low burlesque. Traditionally – insofar as the concept applies to an ideal misplaced for more than a thousand years – caliphs were selected through consultation with honoured scholars, not hoist on the backs of legionnaires, like emperors in ancient Rome. 'The Islamic caliphate cannot be restored by force,' said the Grand Imam of Cairo's Al-Azhar University, Sheikh Abbas Shuman, the foremost interpreter of Sunni doctrine. 'Occupying a country and killing half of its population ... this is not an Islamic state, this is terrorism.'[9]

The subject of manpower was certainly on Abu Bakr's mind on 2 July as he recorded his first radio statement as Caliph Ibrahim. He ordered his listeners to present themselves for service immediately: 'O Muslims everywhere, whoever is capable of performing *hijra* [emigration] to the Islamic State, then let him do so, because *hijra* to the land of Islam is obligatory.' He followed this general call of duty with an extraordinary appeal to scholars, legal experts, judges, military, administrative and service 'specialists', medical doctors and engineers. 'We call them, and remind them to fear Allah, for their *hijra*,' he said.

Abu Bakr was shrewdly aware of competing claims for sacrifice, including those of the Arab Spring; he denounced the 'dazzling and deceptive slogans, such as civilisation, peace, co-existence, freedom, democracy, secularism, Baathism, nationalism and patriotism'. But his overriding objective was to convince thousands of Muslims that a unique spiritual journey was underway and that they all had the right to join in it.

'This is my advice to you. If you hold to it, you will conquer Rome and own the world, if Allah wills.'[10]

* * *

Middlemen at Turkey's Hatay Airport drove Europeans intending to fight to villages like Atmeh, east of the border, a place noted for the giant oak planted to honour a local saint 150 years before. There they could rest, change money, use the internet and savour the pulse of life in a gateway that separated one part of their lives from the beginning of what might be the last.

The war had blessed Atmeh with a twofold business: displaced families travelling north to Olive Tree refugee camp and foreign fighters pausing for breath before continuing south for the final ascent. Like any Himalayan base camp, the menus catered to the diaspora, and shops stocked sun cream, anti-diarrhoeal pills, trail food, sportswear and consumer electronics for the journey to come. The streets were filled with Arab and Afghan fighters on leave from the front, their voices mixing with the accents of London, Paris and Berlin.[11]

No matter what the direction of travel, whoever came to Atmeh was yearning to live life more fully, but whether through political solidarity, religious conviction, self-purification or sheer escape depended on personal circumstances. Syrians were running from the siege on their doorsteps, while Saudis, Tunisians, Moroccans and Jordanians, who came in their thousands, sought to discharge a religious duty by fighting for Sunni freedom or dying in an action to advance the Sunni cause.

Young European Moslems tended to look beyond the sectarian dimension to a blank screen on which to re-invent themselves as samurai in a multi-level contest that played out much like the video game, *Call of Duty*, at least initially. Dismissed in their domestic media as gap-year jihadis, gangsta' converts or misguided punks, they nonetheless shared a dream that enraptured men 20 years more senior, weary of Western comforts – and women who, uniquely in any conflict, were one-in-10 of all Europeans who travelled to enlist.[12]

This widening of the recruitment pool to include bored adolescents and runaway brides – added to easy access to short-haul tourist flights to the killing fields – created consternation in France, UK, Germany and Belgium, the largest European source nations, fearful that their delinquent Muslim youth would return to commit terrorist attacks at home.

There were more than 5,000 foreign fighters in Syria by mid-2013, 1,000 of them from the West, according to one of the many attempts to gauge the size of the problem. That was still a modest amount relative to what it would be a year later, but already more than the 4,000 who went to fight communism in Afghanistan over a 12-year period.[13]

By September 2013, control of Atmeh was divided between four factions: ISIS, JaN, the Army of Emigrants and Helpers, and a second Chechen-led group, Abu al-Binat. JaN only accepted volunteers with letters of reference, who were non-smokers – for 'smoking drives away the angels and delays our victory'.[14] The Chechens only took Russian-speakers: by mid-2014, the 700–1,500 Russian-speakers from the Caucasus, Ukraine and Central Asia constituted the largest group of 'European' fighters in Syria and Iraq.[15]

ISIS became the main beneficiary of the foreign influx, initially by default but later through preference as news spread of its conquests, each rigorously reported through social media. When ISIS took undisputed possession of Atmeh in December 2013, a masked fighter took a chain-saw to the venerable oak, accusing villagers of praying to its branches, rather than to Allah. The senseless beheading sent a wave of despondency across the district.[16]

In his first message as caliph, Abu Bakr had implicitly raised the reward for those who responded to the call of duty with a guarantee that they could settle and reside.

It is a State where the Arab and non-Arab, the white man and black man, the easterner and westerner are all brothers … Therefore, rush O Muslims to your State. Yes, it is your State. Rush, because Syria is not for the Syrians, and Iraq is not for the Iraqis. The earth is Allah's.[17]

Whether this significantly increased Western recruitment is unknown, but the Syrian Observatory for Human Rights claimed that 6,300 new fighters joined in July alone, the month the caliphate was formally declared, of whom 5,300 were Syrians. Other sources reported 1,000 new recruits each month until October, despite the increased danger posed by US air strikes.[18]

Europeans were especially prized, with some in Raqqah earning $800–1,200 per month, paid in dollars, as well as free housing in the former homes of Alawites and Christians. Syrian fighters were paid monthly salaries of at least $300, with additional expenses for wives and children, a package that reflected Abu Bakr's preoccupation with attracting families to the Islamic state. By way of comparison, the Danish Refugee Council offered $50 a month to any Syrian deemed to be in need.[19]

Estimates of IS' total strength, its foreign contingent and the number of Westerners differ widely, from the Soufan Group's total of 12,000 in May 2014, through a CIA calculation of 9,000–18,000 in late 2014, to the 100,000 figure proposed by the Iraqi IS expert, Hisham al-Hashimi, in August 2014. Some go even higher.[20] At least two sources estimate the total number of 'foreign' recruits since January 2013 at 20,000, without specifying whether a Syrian counts as a foreigner.[21]

One analyst reverse-estimated IS manpower based on NATO's experience in Afghanistan whereby 30,000 coalition forces were required imperfectly to subdue 1.6 million people in the provinces of Helmand and Nimroz. Based on this ratio, ISIS would require 30,000 men to stabilise the 2.25 million Syrians within its borders and 45,000 for the 4–4.6 million Iraqi residents – in addition to the number of fighters required for large-scale offensives.[22]

Even by the most generous estimates of the cash held in Mosul's banks, IS was living far beyond its visible means.

17

Inside the Whale

On 4 July, 24 Delta Force commandos landed by helicopter in the small town of Akrishi, three miles south-east of Raqqah, on a secret mission to rescue James Foley, Steven Sotloff and other US hostages held by the IS. Their target was a building described by earlier captives, all of whom had been successfully ransomed: US and British hostages could expect no release because their governments refused to negotiate with kidnappers, often criminalising ransom payments as 'funding terrorism'.

With no monetary value, Foley was subjected to mock execution and crucifixion, and real waterboarding by his guards, a group of British jihadis known as the Beatles. 'We used to call it the Dead Zone when things got bad,' Cantlie wrote later, 'after the area Everest climbers face above 26,000 feet as they approach the summit, when every step is agony, when they hardly have enough strength to carry on.'[1]

As Black Hawk helicopters, F-18 fighters and drones circled overhead, the Delta Force moved stealthily to the house where Foley was believed to be held, only to find it empty: 'dry hole', the commander reported by radio. After a three-hour battle, in which five ISIS fighters were killed, the commandos were extracted to a 'neighbouring country', probably Jordan, ending the only coordinated military response since the fall of Mosul three weeks earlier.

There could be no more striking symbol of a bankrupt policy than the rout of an army the United States had spent $20 billion to build and the loss of enough military kit to equip three full divisions: but was it a Bush or an Obama failure? President Obama had so studiously avoided a repetition of Bush's mistakes in the Middle East that the micro-management he practised via caveats on different actors in the two conflicts ended by strengthening the very force that now threatened to reduce them both to failed states.

Yet US initiatives after Mosul were just as piecemeal and non-confrontational as the policy that preceded it, indicating that Obama remained consistent in his judgement, but anything resembling a realistic strategy to crush IS took three more months to pass a hostile, more hawkish Congress – without convincing the Pentagon, media or Syria's rebels that it stood a chance of success.

The spearhead of US might is its ability to deliver thunderous airstrikes around the clock, but it is manpower, not air power, that ultimately wins wars. If the United States fully intended to hold back from military engagement – 'boots on the ground' – the use of air power risked becoming no more than shallow bombast, disguised as a campaign of attrition.

On 15 June 2014, the president ordered the first of a set of cautious deployments, with the goal of securing the US Embassy in Baghdad and preparing for a full evacuation of staff. On 26 June, 275 advisors were sent to assess the Iraqi army, and lay the basis for improved surveillance and intelligence. By the end of July, the number had risen to 750, a figure that more than quadrupled to 3,000 by November.[2]

In a bid to square the manpower issue, in late June 2014 President Obama requested Congress to approve $500 million to train and arm 15,000 fighters from the Syrian opposition over a three-year period, a bill that was authorised in September. 'In helping those who fight for the right of all Syrians to choose their own future,' he told a West Point audience, 'we also push back against the growing number of extremists who find safe haven in the chaos.' In truth, he was putting the cart before the horse.

The Syrian rebels the United States intended to support were expected to turn their sights on IS, using the weapons systems and air cover Obama had denied them in the unequal battle against the regime – which would naturally thrive from any deflection in their hostile intent. In accepting the US offer, fighters would convert from armed revolutionaries to the Syrian equivalent of the *Sahwa*: defending the same regime that had killed 150,000 of their fellow citizens, and earning the curse of their neighbours.

Signing up to the Obama plan, with no US protection of the kind provided to *Sahwa* during the Iraqi experiment with tribal militias, was a one-way ticket to annihilation. In a dry run of the Obama concept, two moderate groups in Idlib, trained by the United States in Qatar, were quickly targeted by JaN, which looted their US weapons and pushed them across the Turkish border. And what was the United States was offering in return? When asked in November 2014 if he was actively considering Assad's overthrow, President Obama replied: 'We are looking for a political solution eventually in Syria.' This was a poor appetiser for potential allies.[3]

With no prospect of reviving the *Sahwa* in Iraq after al-Malaki's three-year trampling of the Anbar Sunnis, the United States took the least bad option of forcing him from power. Surprisingly, in view of January's loss of Fallujah, al-Malaki had won a reasonable majority and a possible fourth term in the April elections, but after IS' advance as far as Taji, his reputation, and that of his army, were in tatters. Facing criticism from all sides, particularly from Iran, he reluctantly relinquished power on 15 August in favour of Haider al-Abadi, a moderate Shii politician both the United States and Iran could agree upon.

Even as the United States attempted to shape conditions for containing IS, Abu Bakr's fighters were in headlong expansion, buoyed by the triumph in Mosul and speeding towards outflanked enemies in hundreds of looted Humvees, bristling with assault rifles and rocket launchers. The real shape-changer, however, was a fleet of white Toyota Tacoma pick-ups, double-cabbed with mounted machine guns, which IS filmed in multiple parades of black-clad, masked fighters as they drove in formation along desert tracks and city streets.

The vehicles had been specially modified for US Special Forces and were unavailable outside the Toyota assembly plant in San Antonio, Texas: how they managed to reach the frontiers of the caliphate was anyone's guess.[4]

With scarcely a pause, IS started to mop up the last pockets of resistance, a process that looked like a grisly rampage but had the hallmarks of a campaign precisely designed to instil the fear of God in its enemies. In the west, IS launched the largest, anti-regime operation it had undertaken to date: an attack on the Shaer gas field, 45km from Palmyra, which fuels much of Syria's domestic electricity supply. The field's 270 defenders, mostly NDF militia with a sprinkling of civilians, were shot, mutilated, strewn across the desert – and filmed as a warning to others.[5]

Turning north-east, IS forces launched a sequence of attacks to take out the regime's remaining outposts: the 17th Reserve Division, 1km from Raqqah city; the 93rd Brigade, 40km south of the Turkish border; and al-Tabqa airbase, on the shores of Lake Assad. The 17th Division fell after two days' fighting, with the loss of 105 soldiers, but 140 escaped to nearby villages after regime aircraft struck back. IS fighters captured six soldiers inside the base, shot and decapitated them, staking the heads on spiked railings in Paradise Square.[6]

The Syrian campaign continued with an IS attack on the base of the 93rd Brigade in Ayn Isa, which fell after three days, forcing hundreds of defeated troops to seek refuge at al-Tabqa, the regime's last stronghold. After two weeks of fighting, in which 350 IS and 170 Syrian troops were killed, al-Tabqa finally fell on 24 August.

Seven hundred frightened soldiers made it on foot across the desert to Al-Ajrawi, 17 km to the south-west, with IS in pursuit. After three days, several hundred were cornered, stripped naked and force-marched back across the sand to a grain silo, 12km to the north. From there, they were driven 93km east to a site some distance beyond Raqqah. The prisoners dismounted and were ordered onto their stomachs. A dozen fighters opened fire into their bodies.[7]

The high price of resisting IS rule was also made apparent to the Shaitat tribe in the villages of Abu Hamam, between Deir ez-Zour city and the Iraqi border at Al Bukamal. What was variously reported as a failed revolt, a quarrel over public smoking or a Shaitat ambush of an IS patrol led to the bloodiest reprisal of the IS era in early August: over 700 civilians, many as young as 15, were beheaded, shot and crucified in a three-day orgy of killing.[8]

The most detailed account suggests that the killing of an IS militant by a Shaitat tribesman ignited an already volatile situation, providing an opportunity for IS to issue a ruthless example of the fate of any would-be *Sahwa* on both sides of the border. IS reportedly shelled Abu Hamam for three days with artillery hauled in from Mosul, before rounding up the males for execution. Video showed headsmen, mainly Tunisian, Saudi and Egyptian, decapitating the Shaitat prisoners, swinging their severed heads and taunting those in line: 'It's your turn next.'[9]

The first month of Islamist rule in Mosul seemed to show IS behaving with a relatively lighter touch than in Raqqah, with no exemplary executions. Forced to choose between IS and the Shia forces which had abandoned them to its mercy, Mosslawis were minded to give Abu Bakr the benefit of the doubt – until the *al-Hisba* religious guardians began a radical redesign of a skyline that was testimony to Mosul's tolerant past and the fountainhead of its identity.

Four Sunni Sufi shrines, and six Shia mosques were demolished by the first week of July. On 23 July 2014, *al-Hisba* rigged explosives to the mosque at the tomb of the prophet Jonah, revered equally by Jews, Christians and Muslims for being devoured by a whale. A day later, the shrines to the prophets Seth and George were destroyed. 'At first we expected them to only blow up places for Shia people,' said a Mosul official, 'now they are blowing up everything.'[10]

When IS announced that it had plans to blow up the Hadba, a twelfth-century minaret at the Great Mosque, which leans like the Tower of Pisa and adorns the 10,000 dinar banknote, locals formed a human chain to prevent demolition. This act of architectural resistance blossomed into armed opposition in late July with the formation of the Mosul Battalions, which carried out sniper and bomb attacks against IS in units named after the lost monuments of their native city.[11]

On the night of 2 August, the same IS forces that seized Mosul attacked Sinjar, inhabited by Kurdish followers of the Yazidi faith, whom IS scorned as 'peacock worshippers'. There were good military reasons for neutralising the town, then occupied by 250 Kurdish *peshmerga*, since it prevented the link-up between IS territories in Syria and Iraq, but the advance was fired by an ideological hatred, aimed at nothing less than the obliteration of Yazidi culture.

The UN collected evidence from 15 communities, other than Sinjar, where IS had rounded up the Yazidi population, divided it between men and women, and summarily executed all the males. Four hundred were killed in Kocho, 250–300 in Hardan, 200 in Adnaniya: by October 2014, 5,000 Yazidi men were estimated to have been murdered in massacres around Sinjar.[12]

The women were divided into three groups: married with children; married without children; and single women and young girls. IS numbered the single females, and 'inspected them to evaluate their beauty'. Some were given as gifts; some sold for up to $1,000 each; some distributed as lottery prizes; and others 'married' to IS fighters in group ceremonies.[13]

Women and young girls were blindfolded, handcuffed, beaten and repeatedly raped, before being resold. The UN obtained reports of girls as young as six being raped over several days by multiple fighters. An estimated 7,000 Yazidi females were still being held as sex slaves in October.

After the *peshmerga* precipitately withdrew on 3 August, 50,000 Yazidis took refuge on the treeless slopes of Mount Sinjar, bracing for the *coup de grâce*, as the media beamed updates on the 45-degree heat and the refugees' dwindling supplies of water. Four days later, to 'prevent a potential act of genocide', President Obama ordered jets to hit IS convoys and ground positions: a one-day operation, but the first step towards the daily schedule of airstrikes that formed the backbone of Operation Inherent Resolve, the multinational, anti-IS campaign launched a month later – though untitled until October 2014.

Of more practical benefit to the Yazidis was the creation of a safe corridor to Mount Sinjar's northern slopes, which Syrian Kurdish fighters managed to open on 9 August. By the time US marines landed on 13 August to assess the prospects for an evacuation, 35,000 Yazidis had already staggered across the Syrian border after a seven-hour trek, for onward transit to Iraqi Kurdistan.[14]

Media coverage of the plight of the Yazidis dislodged President Obama from his preferred course of indirect intervention in Iraq and Syria and, in turn, brought forward the killing that made direct US action against IS unavoidable.

IS released a video, called 'Message to America', on 19 August 2014 which documented the beheading of photographer James Foley by a British fighter, known as Jihadi John, one of the four 'Beatles' in Raqqah. The Londoner said the execution was revenge for the airstrikes near Sinjar 12 days before, and presented Steven Sotloff, a *Time* stringer, as the next candidate for beheading if the United States did not call them off. 'The life of this American citizen, Obama, depends on your next decision,' he said.

John Cantlie had been moved before Foley's execution to solitary confinement in a 'dark room with a mattress on the floor'. 'I find the close confines of the walls stop my mind wandering too far,' he wrote, 'and I can focus more, keep myself in check in my solitude.'[15]

18

Euphrates Volcano

IS' seizure of the Turkish consulate in Mosul on 10 June 2014, along with its 49 diplomatic staff, compelled Prime Minister Recep Tayyip Erdoğan to address a very awkward question. Which was the greater threat to Turkey's national security: IS or Syria's Kurdish minority?

Abu Bakr seems to have paraphrased this question earlier in March as ISIS forces advanced on the tomb of Suleiman Shah, a twelfth-century tribal leader from Central Asia whose grandson, Osman I, founded the Ottoman empire. Situated in Karakozak, an Aleppo settlement on the west bank of the Euphrates, the mausoleum and its grounds had remained sovereign Turkish territory, 25km inside Syria, since the 1921 Treaty of Ankara, which ceded control of Syria to France as part of the post-Ottoman carve-up.

Owning a revered, historic monument in a war-torn neighbouring state was a mixed blessing for a government that had done so much to stoke the conflict from the outset. Though Suleiman Shah's resting place had never been disturbed in nearly three years of fighting, its inviolability owed less to the resident 40-man military guard, than to Erdoğan's own version of President Obama's 'red-line' threat on the likely US retaliation for use of chemical weapons.

'That tomb and the land around [it],' Erdoğan had warned in August 2012, 'is Turkish territory. We cannot remain idle to anything wrong happening there because that would be an attack against our land. It will also be an attack against NATO territory.'[1]

Mortgaging Turkey's credibility with the defence alliance for a collection of relics was symptomatic of Erdoğan's style, but Suleiman Shah continued to serve Ankara's purpose 900 years after his death by providing a pretext for cross-border interference against the Assad regime, whenever it was needed.

In the two weeks prior to the ISIS advance, Ankara had authorised military action to defend the tomb from attack and shot down a Syrian jet, which it claimed violated Turkish airspace near Latakia province. In the last days of March, a video, allegedly circulated by IS, warned: 'We are giving you three days [to evacuate] the soldiers in this tomb, which is on the Islamic land of Aleppo, or we will raze the tomb.'[2]

With its well-established hatred of shrines, the ISIS threat seemed credible, but on 27 March YouTube posted a recording of a national security meeting in which senior Turkish officials conspired to manufacture a military incident to justify an invasion of northern Syria, using Suleiman Shah's grave as *casus belli*.

Referring to the ISIS advance, Foreign Minister Ahmet Davutoğlu is heard to say: 'The prime minister said that in the current conjuncture, this attack must be seen as an opportunity for us.' To which Hakan Fidan, head of Turkey's MIT intelligence agency, responds:

Now look, my commander, if there is to be justification, the justification is, I send four men to the other side. I get them to fire eight missiles into empty land. That's not a problem. Justification can be created [...] We can also prepare an attack on Suleiman Shah Tomb if necessary.

Erdoğan did not deny the recording's authenticity, but blocked access to YouTube for two months.[3]

The ISIS threat never materialised but it may not have been genuine in the first place, given the easily fabricated evidence of a single menacing video. The group's military dependence on Turkey's permissive border policy for an uninterrupted flow of recruits into Syria, as well as whatever arms, money and other supplies managed to cross, would have made such a provocation counter-productive indeed. 'Turkey is to Syria now what Pakistan was to Afghanistan in the 1990s,' said Thomas Hegghammer, a Norwegian specialist of jihadi groups. There was nothing to be gained from IS attacking a compliant neighbour.[4]

Evidence of more committed Turkish assistance specifically to ISIS prior to the fall of Mosul is anecdotal, reflecting the country's virulently polarised political environment. In January 2014, a search by gendarmes of three MIT trucks allegedly carrying aid from Ankara airport to Reyhanli on the Syrian border revealed containers filled with missiles, mortar shells and anti-aircraft ammunition. Though the incident spiralled into a public spat between the two security services which eventually smeared Prime Minister Erdoğan, the consignee was most likely Ahrar al-Sham, which controlled the relevant border crossing, rather than ISIS as was widely reported at the time.[5]

Numerous related allegations, including medical treatment of ISIS fighters in Turkish hospitals, the hosting of training camps and the facilitation of local recruitment, all fall short of qualifying as a coordinated programme of clandestine Turkish support to ISIS, but there were two areas where there was an indisputable meeting of minds.[6]

The first was oil, which ISIS had in abundance since conquering Raqqah and Deir ez-Zour, but Syrian rebels had been smuggling by pipeline since 2011. 'They run through fields and under the stone streets of the town and come out in the back courtyards of local houses,' reported Fehim Taştekin from Hacıpaşa in Hatay for *Radikal*. 'The oil is pumped from the other side and fills storage tanks in these courtyards. [...] This is the prize for local villagers who support the state's Syria policy.'[7]

Smuggled diesel sold for around one-third of official prices, and one opposition MP claimed ISIS was trading up to 4,000 tonnes every day in Turkey, earning $15 million per month. By mid-2014, IS territory in Iraq was capable of producing 25,000–40,000 barrels a day, vastly amplifying those estimates in theory, but Turkish gendarmes had received orders by March to tear up the make-shift pipelines.[8]

The second area of common interest was the Kurdish population of northern Syria, the only barrier to the caliphate's expansion to the north, and equally a thorn in Erdoğan's side. Assad removed Syrian forces from most Kurdish areas in July 2012 in exchange for a non-aggression pact with the dominant Democratic Union Party (PYD), led by Saleh Muslim Muhammed, and its People's Defence Units (YPG).

Both the PYD and YPG are offshoots of Turkey's Kurdistan Workers' Party (PKK), a Marxist-Leninist movement which waged a long and violent struggle for an independent Kurdish state until the arrest of its founder and chief ideologue, Abdullah Öcalan, in 1999. Two years before that, the United States designated it a terrorist organisation, more to please a vital NATO ally than from any direct threat to US interests.

From his prison cell, Öcalan had since repudiated the objective of an independent united Kurdistan in favour of Kurdish self-determination within the existing national frontiers of Turkey, Iran, Iraq and Syria. Assad's military withdrawal from his Kurdish enclaves on the Turkish border mischievously revived Öcalan's fading dream just as Ankara seemed in reach of a peace settlement.[9]

In late 2013, the PYD announced the birth of Rojava, or Western Kurdistan, a multi-ethnic region of Kurds, Arabs and Christians ruled along secular and democratic lines, according to Öcalan's revised teachings. One visitor, journalist Patrick Cockburn, said it was the 'only place in Syria where the original progressive aims of the uprising of 2011 [had] been achieved at least in part'. Divided into the non-contiguous cantons of Afrin, Kobane and Jazira, Rojava has scarcely two million people, but 60 per cent of Syria's oil reserves.[10]

Its chances of survival were dim for Rojava's very existence attracted the enmity of JaN, ISIS, Ahrar al-Sham, the FSA, Turkey and, for entirely different reasons, Iraqi Kurdistan. YPG militias refused to participate in the FSA, arguing it was a Turkish cartel that served Turkish interests, and in May 2013, the leaders of 21 armed groups denounced Kurds as 'traitors to the jihad', threatening a 'cleansing process' of Kurds and *shabiha*, shorthand for Assad militia. Meanwhile, Turkey hoped to speed Rojava's downfall by allowing JaN forces to transit its territory to fight the YPG in the eastern canton of Jazira.[11]

By the time Mosul fell to ISIS on 11 June 2014, JaN, Ahrar al-Sham and the FSA were no longer the significant actors they once had been in the vast tracts of Syria now controlled by the Iraqi-led group, re-branded IS. Indeed, Turkey had taken the decision one week earlier to designate JaN, its former partner, as an Al Qaeda-linked group in a belated gesture to the United States.[12]

After declaring his caliphate in the Grand Mosque in early July, Abu Bakr was whisked away to the captured Turkish Consulate, now re-purposed as IS headquarters. 'It is their office', said former governor Atheel al-Nujaifi, whose advice days earlier to evacuate the 49 hostages, including diplomats' wives and children, was rejected by Foreign Minister Ahmet

Davutoğlu. With 31 truck drivers seized later, IS had 80 reasons why Prime Minister Erdoğan should pay close attention to its demands. Some analysts considered Turkey itself had been overpowered.[13]

IS began moving captured Iraqi T-55 tanks, artillery and troop transports to Syria's Al-Hasakeh province within a week of Mosul falling. By mid-July, 800 members of the PKK had crossed the Turkish border to join the YPG in Kobane (Ayn al-Arab, in Arabic), the central of Rojava's three cantons, to celebrate the second anniversary of Kurdish liberation from Syrian rule, with 1,000 more predicted to follow. 'Kobane has become the new rallying point for the Kurds,' said a journalist in Diyarbakir, 'and most believe that Turkey is helping [IS].'[14]

A former construction camp on the Berlin–Baghdad railway, which demarcates this part of the Turkish frontier, Kobane's only strategic value was its border crossing, which had been locked since Ankara imposed an embargo on Rojava. IS controlled two other crossings at Jarablus and Tal Abyad, so no obvious purpose was served in attacking the canton, other than to inflict an exemplary defeat on the YPG of the type it had served on JaN, the FSA, the Iraqi army and the Shaitat tribe.

If there were a relaxed swagger to the IS advance, it seemed justified by the threat to the Turkish hostages, now moved to Raqqah. Their uncertain destiny was guaranteed to delay any adverse reaction from Ankara, even if it were so inclined, or at least justify Turkish efforts to rein in its NATO allies, at a time when Erdoğan was also seeking election as president. These calculations had to be readjusted in early August, when President Obama ordered airstrikes in Iraq to protect the Yazidis on Mount Sinjar, signalling a willingness to broaden the air campaign if pushed. Nevertheless, IS pressed on.

On 13 September, IS launched a major offensive into the eastern and western flanks of Kobane canton, capturing scores of villages and forcing 45,000 people to flee. It was the start of a 135-day battle that would drive most of Kobane's population into exile, ruin 80 per cent of its capital, but end with the victorious YPG raising a 75-metre Kurdish flag above Mistenour Hill, in open scorn of the Turkish tanks that had gazed stonily on the siege throughout.[15]

The Turkish hostages were released a week after the offensive began, reportedly in exchange for 180 IS fighters held by groups linked to the FSA, although now-President Erdoğan denied any such trade had taken place. 'If they are referring to financial bargaining, this is out of the question,' he said. 'But if they are referring to a diplomatic bargaining, of course we are talking about a political, diplomatic bargaining.' A Turkish website linked to IS called the discussions over the hostages 'a phase of negotiations, held basically between two states'.[16]

Though now freed from its hostage burden, Turkey refused to participate in airstrikes launched against IS positions around Kobane on 27 September 2014 by the United States, Saudi Arabia and United Arab Emirates, denying them access or refuelling rights at Incirlik military airport. 'Saving Kobane is very important,' said new Prime Minister Ahmet Davutoğlu, formerly the foreign minister, in October, 'but we should not forget that Kobane is just a result of a much bigger, much more widespread crisis in Syria.'[17]

He insisted that the US take military action against the Assad regime and impose a no-fly zone over northern Syria before making Incirlik available to coalition jets. Allegations of direct Turkish assistance to IS had continued to circulate, notably from Anwar Moslem, mayor of Kobane, who reported trainloads of fighters and ammunition making lengthy, unscheduled halts at village stations east of Kobane. 'There are evidences, witnesses and videos about this,' he said, 'why is [IS] strong only in Kobane's east?'[18]

Nevertheless, a day after the prime minister's insistence that the US deploy firepower against Assad's forces, he authorised the transit through Turkey of 200 FSA and Iraqi Kurdish fighters, who reinforced the Kobane garrison on 29 October bringing heavy weapons and ammunition with them. Despite the token quantity involved, it was clear that Turkey had crossed a bridge in regard to IS.

A month after the YPG declared victory at Kobane, a Turkish convoy of 39 tanks and 57 armoured vehicles, carrying over 500 troops, drove through the shattered remains of the canton on a mission to rescue the honour guard at the tomb of Suleiman Shah and remove his remains to a safer location – closer to the Turkish border but still in Syria. Turkish officials said the relics would be returned to its previous location in Karakozak at a later date, and that Turkey continued to claim the land.[19]

Postscript
Saddam's Ghost

'O America, O allies of America, and O crusaders,' warned Abu Muhammad al-Adnani in a keynote speech on 21 September 2014, titled 'Indeed your Lord is ever watchful'. 'Know that the matter is more dangerous than you have imagined and greater than you have envisioned [...] We will conquer your Rome, break your crosses, and enslave your women, by the permission of Allah.'[1]

Eleven days earlier, President Obama had announced his intention to 'degrade and ultimately destroy' IS through a campaign of air strikes forming part of Operation Inherent Resolve, in which the air forces of 20 states would eventually participate. Since the fall of Mosul, the United States had conducted air strikes on its own, primarily to relieve pressure on Iraqi or Kurdish forces around Kirkuk, Irbil, Baghdad and Sinjar.[2]

Obama's announcement indicated a broadening of that effort to include allies in the Gulf and NATO against IS targets in Syria, including Raqqah, the capital of the caliphate, Kobane, and as far west as Aleppo where 'Khorasan', a hitherto unknown Al Qaeda special forces group operating under the protection of JaN was reportedly planning terrorist operations against the West.[3]

Coordinating such a coalition entailed careful parsing of national caveats: Saudi Arabia and the United Arab Emirates collaborated with the United States on attacking IS assets around Kobane, but refused to rescue Iraq's Shia regime, while Qatar pleaded a previous engagement. A House of Commons ruling precluded UK air operations in Syria, but freed it to use Tornados and Reaper drones over Kurdish Iraq. Aside from the United States, only Canada was at liberty to conduct strikes in both sectors of the Islamic state's borders.[4]

Al-Adnani's words were chosen to inspire the hundreds of fighters soon to lose their lives in the bombing campaign in Kobane, but they also turned the screw on Obama's long-standing refusal to respond to Syria's civil war atrocities or the abuses of Sunni rights by the US-installed al-Maliki government in Iraq, both of which had hotly divided Washington from its Gulf partners since the withdrawal of US forces from the region in December 2011.

Al-Adnani continued,

> [America's] sentiments were not stirred during the long years of siege and starvation in Sham, and looked the other way when the deadly and destructive barrel bombs were being dropped. It was not outraged when it saw the horrific scenes of the women and children of the Muslims taking their last breaths with their eyes glazed over due to the chemical weapons of the *nusayriyyah* (Alawites) – scenes which continue to be repeated every day.
>
> [...] But when a state emerged for the Muslims that would defend them, take revenge for them, and carry out retribution, America and the crusaders started shedding crocodile tears for the sake of a few hundred *rafidi* [Shia] and *nusayriyyah* criminal soldiers that IS had taken as prisoners of war and executed. The hearts of America and its allies were broken by the IS when it cut off the rotten heads of some agents, spies and apostates.

It was not a subtle argument, but it contained a grain of truth given Iraqi civilian deaths of 162,000–500,000 from

2003–2013 and 190,000 in Syria since March 2011. The first resulted from President George Bush's imperial interference in the sectarian balancing act in Iraq under Saddam Hussein; the latter from President's Barack Obama's horrified reaction to its consequences, and his unyielding resolution to say 'never again'. By contrast, IS was reportedly responsible for 8,493 civilian deaths in the first eight months of 2014, with more than half occurring from 1 June to 31 August.[5]

Yet when Obama did change his mind, it was to protect the Yezidis on Mount Sinjar and reverse IS' territorial gains in Iraq, not to relieve the districts of Damascus, Aleppo or Idlib where Syrian forces had been starving greater numbers of civilians for years. Obama's decision to launch air strikes against IS seemed reactive to current news events, rather than preventive for the region in the long term. In short, it looked cynical.

The air strikes launched against IS in Kobane on 27 September were exercises in public affairs, more than plans calculated to achieve specific military goals. Secretary of State John Kerry was quite blunt: 'Kobane does not define the strategy for the coalition in respect to [IS].'[6] First, they were unleashed two weeks after IS started its own offensive, allowing fighters to embed deep in the downtown area, which forced the YPG to engage in desperate house-to-house fighting before finally expelling them. Second, they were timed to allow Turkey to complete negotiations over the safe release of its consular hostages from Mosul.

Certainly, television footage of air strikes from journalists camped out overlooking Kobane gave a visual impression of Obama's determination to crush IS, but the fact that the siege lasted four-and-a-half months and that the raids produced so few tangible results – beyond the basic psychological victory of forcing IS to make a tactical withdrawal – gave the lie to the air campaign's ultimate value. 'It's tactically, momentarily relevant,' said Christopher Harmer, a former pilot working for the Institute for the Study of War, 'and strategically incoherent.'[7]

After 10 weeks of strikes in Iraq and Syria by 100 bombers, fighters, attack helicopters and drones, the combined might of 20 air forces had eliminated 280 trucks, 54 looted Humvees, 120 buildings, 48 'fighting positions', 27 checkpoints, 28 tanks and 19 artisanal oil refineries, while IS casualties in Kobane were estimated in the high hundreds. It was hardly a display of the 'shock and awe' over Baghdad that preceded the 2003 land invasion, whose bluster was only too familiar to the veteran Iraqi officers and AQI insurgents who commanded IS at Kobane.[8]

'Air power needs to be applied like a thunderstorm,' said the three-star general who planned the air campaigns in the 1991 Gulf War and the 2001 invasion of Afghanistan, 'and so far we've witnessed only a drizzle.' By 9 November, only 800 of 3,200 flights had found worthy targets to justify releasing their payloads, forcing three-quarters to return to their Gulf bases with bomb-bays intact.[9]

Analysts blamed the poverty of targets, lack of forward spotting teams or the built-in constraints of air power when used as a primary tool against militant networks, without a ground force to deliver the death blow, but the more obvious explanation for Inherent Resolve's failure was political. The president had no commitment to fighting IS tooth and nail as long as it confined its attacks to abusive rhetoric, butchering journalists or targeting religious minorities.[10]

These were insufficient challenges to national security to justify putting American boots on the ground or – the only other option seemingly available – US recognition of the Assad regime as its only viable partner to defeat IS in the field. There were no other fighting forces to work with in Iraq or Syria, aside from the Kurds, who only fought beyond their contested borders to aggrandise more of their historic terrain, and collaboration with whom risked pushing Washington ever deeper into a rift with Turkey.

Any other alternative force would have to be built from scratch, with no guarantee of more decisive performance than the Iraqi security forces, which had taken the United States 10 years to train and arm, but which folded within hours of the enemy's approach. Yet that was precisely the route the United States chose to follow. Kerry said,

> We have said from day one that it is going to take a period of time to bring the coalition thoroughly to the table to rebuild some of the morale and capacity of the Iraqi army. And to begin the focus of where we ought to be focusing first, which is in Iraq. That is the current strategy.[11]

After so many 'red lines' had been drawn in Syria, Obama's options were reduced to a series of short-term policy snacks, each carrying the risk of political embarrassment or diplomatic indigestion – except for one. Over the years Iran's financial and strategic support for bin Laden's Al Qaeda, al-Zarqawi's AQI, al-Maliki's Iraq, Lebanon's Hezbollah and the Assad regime in Syria had maintained the region in a permanent state of violent tension, but Iran, ironically, also offered the chance of a historic agreement – like the US–Russian deal on Syria's chemical weapons, but this time over the quasi-symbolic issue of Tehran's nuclear capability – which could lead to cooperation over a raft of live and semi-frozen conflicts, including with Israel and Saudi Arabia.

According to this line of reasoning, the IS threat to the Sykes–Picot agreement and the civilians of Syria, Iraq, Yemen, Libya and other countries consumed in its rampage, is a transitional, almost exemplary aberration that illustrates just how the region might degenerate without a landmark agreement between the United States and Iran, that would form the keystone of the Obama legacy while offering a face-saving explanation for the absence of decisive US policy in the Middle East over the previous five years.

Saudi Arabia, Syria, Iraq and many other countries, and their fractious, violated populations, might all draw hope from a genuine Persian Spring, but this can only happen if negotiations with Iran take precedence over US action in the civil wars and insurgencies that in one way or another issue from the historic rupture between Washington and Tehran.

In the same way that the US invasion of Iraq was a wasteful diversion from Afghanistan that allowed Al Qaeda to metastise across the world, so concentrating on IS at this time could come at the expense of the lasting achievements that meaningful detente with Tehran might ultimately bring. That is one way to understand President Obama's cosmetic efforts to extinguish IS, arm an effective Syrian rebel front able to defeat Assad's forces, or drive the regime into meaningful power-sharing negotiations.

Another is the so-called 'Blood Borders' map, published by Lt. Col. Ralph Peters in *Armed Forces Journal* in June 2006, which re-imagined the boundaries of the Middle East and South Asia as if delineated according to its 'organic' frontiers, rather than the 'colossal, man-made deformities' of the Sykes–Picot agreement.[12]

In Peters' map, Turkey, Syria, Iraq and Iran lose wide swathes of territory to the new state of Kurdistan; Iran, Afghanistan and Pakistan, shorn of Baluchi lands, shift their centres of gravity to the east. What remains of Iraq is divided into a Shia south and Sunni north, the latter expanded to gobble up eastern Syria along the same borders delineated by the Islamic state. Saudi Arabia, Israel, the United Arab Emirates, Qatar and Kuwait are also big losers in this return to the organic borders of faith and ethnicity.

The Pentagon has been 'gaming' the Peters' map since 2006 in the conviction that a known unknown might still be manageable. IS provides a practical example of how the Sykes–Picot settlement may look if its most powerful legatee nations do not cease their struggle for regional domination along the sectarian fault line of Sunni and Shia.

The survival of IS within the boundaries of the world's newest unrecognised state may, to that extent, serve a higher political purpose than is immediately obvious. One cannot reliably argue that IS was a military and religious entity manufactured specifically to change the region's sectarian borders, but it may end by manufacturing a new consensus between bitter sectarian foes that Sykes–Picot is ultimately preferable to the Blood Borders map of the Middle East.

Notes

Preface

1. Yasmine Ryan, Kairouan, 'Whole World Can Witness My Love of Jihad', *Sunday Times*, 28 June 2015.

1. The Great Escape

1. Ashraf Khalil, 'Camp Bucca Turns 180 Degrees from Abu Ghraib', *Los Angeles Times*, 19 January 2005.
2. John Blosser, 'Iraq War Vet: US Camps Became "Terrorist Universities" for ISIS', *Newsmax*, 16 October 2014.
3. Martin Chulov, 'ISIS: The Inside Story', *Guardian*, 11 December 2014.
4. Amit R. Paley, 'In Iraq, "A Prison Full of Innocent Men"', *Washington Post*, 6 December 2008.
5. Vasilios Tasikas, 'The Battlefield Inside the Wire: Detention Operations Under Major General Douglas Stone', *Military Review*, Vol. 89, No. 5, September–October 2009.
6. Jeffrey Azarva, 'Is U.S. Detention Policy in Iraq Working?' *Middle East Quarterly*, Vol. 16, No. 1, Winter 2009.
7. 'US Iraq Jail an "al-Qaeda School"', *Al Jazeera*, 12 December 2009.
8. Ibid.
9. David Enders, 'Camp Bucca: Iraq's Guantanamo', *The Nation*, 17 October 2008.
10. Chulov, 'ISIS: The Inside Story'.
11. Tim Arango and Eric Schmitt, 'US Actions in Iraq Fueled Rise of a Rebel', *New York Times*, 10 August 2014.
12. Ruth Sherlock, 'How a Talented Footballer Became the World's Most Wanted Man, Abu Bakr al-Baghdadi', *Daily Telegraph*, 11 November 2014.
13. 'ISIS Leader: "See You in New York"', *Daily Beast*, 14 June 2014.
14. Chulov, 'ISIS: The Inside Story'.
15. Ibid.
16. 'A Biography of Abu Bakr al-Baghdadi', *INSITE BLOG on Terrorism and Extremism*, 12 August 2014, at: http://tinyurl.com/koypuzk

17. 'A Biography of Abu Bakr al-Baghdadi'; Aryn Baker, 'Iraqi Government Releases New Photo of the Middle East's Most Wanted Terrorist', *Time*, 23 February 2014.

18. Ala'a Walid, 'Profile: Mysterious "Caliph" Abu Bakr al-Baghdadi', *Middle East Monitor*, 1 July 2014.

19. English Translation of @Wikibaghdady, collected by Yousef Bin Tashfin, at: http://justpaste.it/e90q

20. Adam Strickland, 'Here is the Finalized OSC Translation of AQ Loyalist Abu Ahmad's Account of ISIL and its Origins', *Fund for Fallen Allies*, 25 September 2014, at: http://tinyurl.com/qa3eukq

2. Zarqawi's War

1. Musab al-Zarqawi 'Letter from Musab al-Zarqawi to Osama bin Laden', Council on Foreign Relations, 1 February 2004, at: www.cfr.org/iraq/letter-abu-musab-al-zarqawi-osama-bin-laden/p9863

2. Ibid.

3. Abu Musab al-Zarqawi, 'Zarqawi's Cry', *National Review*, 12 February 2004.

4. Bill Roggio, 'Saif al-Adel, Zarqawi, al Qaeda and Iran', *Long War Journal*, 16 June 2005.

5. Kenneth Katzman, 'Al Qaeda in Iraq: Assessment and Outside Links', Congressional Report Services, 15 August 2008.

6. Roggio, 'Saif al-Adel, Zarqawi, al Qaeda and Iran'.

7. Christopher M. Blanchard, 'Al Qaeda: Statements and Evolving Ideology', Congressional Report Services, 9 July 2007.

8. Raymond Bonner and Joel Brinkley, 'The Struggle for Iraq: The Attackers; Latest Attacks Underscore Differing Intelligence Estimates of Strength of Foreign Guerrillas', *New York Times*, 28 October 2003.

9. Gary Gambill, 'Abu Musab al-Zarqawi: A Biographical Sketch', *Terrorism Monitor*, Vol. 2, No. 24, 15 December 2004.

10. Bill Roggio, 'US Strike in Syria "Decapitated" al Qaeda's Facilitation Network', *Long War Journal*, 27 October 2008.

11. Bill Roggio, 'Iraq Attacks and the Syrian Connection', *Long War Journal*, 30 August 2009.

12. Brian Fishman and Joseph Felter, 'Al-Qa'ida's Foreign Fighters in Iraq: A First Look at the Sinjar Records', Combating Terrorism Center at West Point, 2 January 2007, at: http://tinyurl.com/o69o5l8

13. Thomas Joscelyn, 'Slain Syrian Official Supported al Qaeda in Iraq', *Long War Journal*, 24 July 2012.

14. Susan B. Glasser and Steve Coll, 'The Web as Weapon', *Washington Post*, 9 August 2005.

15. Glasser and Coll, 'The Web as Weapon'; Bill Roggio, 'Senior Syrian al Qaeda Leader Confirmed Killed', *Long War Journal*, 4 December 2007.

16. US State Department, 'Country Reports on Terrorism', 2006, at: www.state.gov/j/ct/rls/crt/2006/

17. Thomas E. Ricks, 'Military Plays Up Role of Zarqawi', *Washington Post*, 10 April 2006.

18. Roggio, 'Saif al-Adel, Zarqawi, al-Qaeda and Iran'.

19. Thomas Joscelyn, 'Analysis: Al Qaeda's Interim Emir and Iran', *Long War Journal*, 18 May 2011.

20. 'Scores Killed in Baghdad Attacks', BBC News, 14 September 2005.

21. Jeffrey Pool, 'Zarqawi's Pledge of Allegiance to Al Qaeda: From Mu'asker Al-Battar', Jamestown Foundation, Vol. 2, No. 24, 16 December 2004.

22. Cited in Maj. Gary W. Brock Jr., 'Zarqawi's Sfumato: Operational Art in IrregularWarfare', at: www.dtic.mil/dtic/tr/fulltext/u2/a583822.pdf; and Michael Eisenstadt and Jeffrey White, 'Assessing Iraq's Sunni Arab Insurgency', *Military Review*, May–June 2006.

23. 'Letter from al-Zawahiri to al-Zarqawi', Global Security, at: http://tinyurl.com/9zujp; Bill Roggio, 'Dear Zarqawi: A Letter from Zawahiri, and a Constitutional Compromise', *Long War Journal*, 12 October 2005.

24. Emily Hunt, 'Zarqawi's "Total War" on Iraqi Shiites Exposes a Divide among Sunni Jihadists', The Washington Institute, 15 November 2005, at: http://tinyurl.com/oydzbxu

25. Blanchard, 'Al Qaeda: Statements and Evolving Ideology'.

26. Ishaan Tharoor, 'Al-Qaeda's Alleged New Leader: Who is Saif al-Adel?' *Time*, 17 May 2011; Joscelyn, 'Analysis: Al Qaeda's Interim Emir and Iran'.

3. *The First Caliph*

1. Valentinas Mite, 'Some Insurgents in Iraq Say They Are Ready to Disarm', Radio Free Europe/Radio Liberty, 8 June 2005.

2. Sabrina Tavernise and Dexter Filkins, 'Local Insurgents Tell of Clashes with Al Qaeda's Forces in Iraq', *New York Times*, 12 January 2006.

3. Bill Roggio, 'US Forces Capture Key Zarqawi Commander', *Long War Journal*, 16 June 2005.

4. Todd Pitman, 'Sunni Sheikhs Join Fight vs. Insurgency', *Associated Press*, 25 March 2007.

5. Mahan Abedin, 'Mujahideen Shura Council in Iraq: Fact or Fiction?', *Terrorism Focus*, Vol. 3, No. 12, Jamestown Foundation, 28 March 2006.

6. 'A Biography of Abu Bakr al-Baghdadi', *INSITE BLOG on Terrorism and Extremism*, 12 August 2014, at: http://tinyurl.com/koypuzk

7. Andrew Tilghman, 'The Myth of AQI', *Washington Monthly*, 10 July 2007, at: www.washingtonmonthly.com/features/2007/0710.tilghman. html

8. Vali Nasr, *The Shia Revival: How Conflicts within Islam Will Shape the Future* (New York: W. W. Norton, 2006).

9. Ellen Knickmeyer, 'Wikileaks Exposes Rumsfeld's Lies', *Daily Beast*, 25 October 2010.

10. Andrew Buncombe and Patrick Cockburn, 'Iraq Cracks: And Now Come the Death Squads', *CounterPunch*, 27 February 2008.

11. Joel Wing, 'Columbia University Charts Sectarian Cleansing of Baghdad', *Musings on Iraq*, 19 November 2009, at: http://musingsoniraq.blogspot. co.uk/2009/11/blog-post.html

12. 'How Zarqawi was Found and Killed', BBC News, 9 June 2006; Ellen Knickmeyer and Jonathan Finer, 'Insurgent Leader Al-Zarqawi Killed in Iraq', *Washington Post*, 8 June 2006.

13. Michael Scheuer, 'Bin Laden Seizes Opportunities in his June and July Speeches', *Terrorism Focus*, Vol. 3, No. 26, Jamestown Foundation, 9 July 2006.

14. Benjamin Bahney, Howard J. Shatz, Carroll Ganier, Renny McPherson, Barbara Sude with Sara Beth Elson and Ghassan Schbley, 'An Economic Analysis of the Financial Records of al-Qa'ida in Iraq', RAND Corporation, 2010.

15. Bill Roggio, 'Dear Zarqawi: A Letter from Zawahiri and a Constitutional Compromise', *Long War Journal*, 12 October 2005; Brian Fishman, 'Dysfunction and Decline: Lessons Learned from Inside Al-Qa'ida in Iraq', Harmony Project, Combating Terrorism Center at West Point, 16 March 2009.

16. Fishman, 'Dysfunction and Decline'; Michael Ware 'Papers Give a Peek Inside Al Qaeda in Iraq', CNN, 11 June 2008.

17. Adam Strickland, 'Here is the Finalized OSC Translation of AQ Loyalist Abu Ahmad's Account of ISIL and its Origins', *Fund for Fallen Allies*, 25 September 2014, at: http://tinyurl.com/qa3eukq

18. 'Report: True Identity of "Islamic State of Iraq" Leader Revealed, Photos Aired', CBS News, 7 May 2008.

19. Dean Yates, 'Senior Qaeda Figure in Iraq a Myth: U.S. Military', *Reuters*, 18 July 2007.

20. Brian Fishman, 'After Zarqawi: The Dilemmas and Future of Al Qaeda in Iraq', *Washington Quarterly*, Vol. 29, No. 4, August 2006.

21. Jesmeen Khan, 'The Iraqi Tribal Structure: Background and Influence on Counter-Terrorism', *Perspectives on Terrorism*, Vol. 1, No. 1, 2007.

22. Norman Cigar, *Al-Qaida, the Tribes and the Government: Lessons and Prospects for Iraq's Unstable Triangle*, Middle East Studies Occasional Papers, No. 2 (Quantico, VA: Marine Corps University Press, 2011).

23. Joel Wing, 'Anbar Before and After the Awakening Part IX: Sheikh Sabah Aziz of the Albu Mahal', *Musings on Iraq*, 23 January 2014.

24. Bahney *et al.*, 'An Economic Analysis of the Financial Records of al-Qa'ida in Iraq'.

25. Kimberly Kagan, 'The Anbar Awakening: Displacing al Qaeda from Its Stronghold in Western Iraq', Institute for the Study of War, 21 August 2006.

26. Joshua Partlow, Ann Scott Tyson and Robin Wright, 'Bomb Kills a Key Sunni Ally of U.S.', *Washington Post*, 14 September 2007; Bahney *et al.*, 'An Economic Analysis of the Financial Records of al-Qa'ida in Iraq'.

27. Kagan, 'The Anbar Awakening'; Bahney *et al.*, 'An Economic Analysis of the Financial Records of al-Qa'ida in Iraq'.

28. Bahney *et al.*, 'An Economic Analysis of the Financial Records of al-Qa'ida in Iraq'.

29. Khan, 'The Iraqi Tribal Structure'.

30. Greg Bruno, 'Finding a Place for the "Sons of Iraq"', Council on Foreign Relations, 9 January 2009.

4.   Clear, Hold and Build

1. Norman Cigar, *Al-Qaida, the Tribes and the Government: Lessons and Prospects for Iraq's Unstable Triangle*, Middle East Studies Occasional Papers, No. 2 (Quantico, VA: Marine Corps University Press, 2011), p. 49.

2. Jim Garamone, 'Terrorists Using Chlorine Car Bombs to Intimidate Iraqis', American Forces Press Service, 6 June 2007.

3. Kimberly Kagan, 'The Anbar Awakening: Displacing al Qaeda from Its Stronghold in Western Iraq', Institute for the Study of War, 21 August 2006.

4. Eric Hamilton, 'The Fight for Mosul: March 2003–March 2008', Institute for the Study of War.

5. Kagan, 'The Anbar Awakening'.

6. U.S. Department of Defense, 'Special Briefing with Multinational Corps-Iraq Commander, Lt. Gen Ray Odierno', 22 June 2007.

7. Bill Roggio, 'Analysis: ISIS, Allies Reviving "Baghdad Belts" Battle Plan', *Long War Journal*, 14 June 2014; 'Baghdad Belts', Institute for the Study of War, at: www.understandingwar.org/region/baghdad-belts

8. Kimberly Kagan, 'The Real Surge: Preparing for Operation Phantom Thunder', Institute for the Study of War.

9. Ibid.

10. 'The Baghdad "Surge" and Civilian Casualties', Iraq Body Count, at: www.iraqbodycount.org/analysis/numbers/baghdad-surge/

11. 'Operation Iraqi Freedom', at: http://icasualties.org/IRAQ/index.aspx

12. Joel Wing, 'The Demise, But Not the Death of Al Qaeda in Iraq', *Musings on Iraq*, 19 June 2008.

13. Bernhard Zand, 'Al-Qaida Versus The Islamic Army: Insurgents in Iraq Turn on Each Other', *Spiegel Online*, 12 June 2007.

14. Michael Knights, 'Lessons from Mosul', Washington Institute, 27 January 2005; Hamilton, 'The Fight for Mosul'.

15. Solomon Moore, 'In Mosul, New Test of Iraqi Army', *New York Times*, 20 March 2008.

16. Sandro Magister, 'Kurdistan's Twin Towers: The Massacre of the Yazidi', *Chiesa*, 24 August 2007, at: chiesa.espresso.repubblica.it/articolo/162781?eng=y

17. Hamilton, 'The Fight for Mosul'.

18. Bill Murray, 'Mosul Conflict Ebbs after Five-Year Battle between Coalition, Insurgents for Control', *Long War Journal*, 24 July 2008.

19. Murray, 'Mosul Conflict Ebbs after Five-Year Battle between Coalition, Insurgents for Control'; and Bill Roggio, Daveed Gartenstein-Ross and Tony Badran, 'Intercepted Letters from al-Qaeda Leaders Shed Light on State of Network in Iraq', Foundation for Defense of Democracies, 12 September 2008.

20. Ibid.

5. *The Successions*

1. 'Documented Civilian Deaths from Violence', Iraq Body Count, at: www.iraqbodycount.org/database/

2. Dr Michael Knights, 'The Resurgence of Al Qaeda in Iraq', Washington Institute for Near East Policy, 21 December 2013.

3. Bill Roggio, 'Al Qaeda in Iraq is "Broken," Cut Off from Leaders in Pakistan, Says Top US General', *Long War Journal*, 5 June 2010.

4. Knights, 'The Resurgence of Al Qaeda in Iraq'.

5. 'Iraqi Deaths from Violence in 2010', Iraq Body Count, at: www.iraqbodycount.org/analysis/numbers/2010/

6. David Ignatius, 'Behind the Carnage in Baghdad', *Washington Post*, 25 August 2009.

7. David Enders, 'Camp Bucca: Iraq's Guantanamo', *The Nation*, 17 October 2008.

8. Anthony Shadid, 'In Iraq, Chaos Feared as US Closes Prison', *Washington Post*, 22 March 2009; Rania Abouzeid, 'In the Waterfront: The U.S. Prison for Iraq's Worst', *Time*, 15 March 2009.

9. Norman Cigar, *Al-Qaida, the Tribes and the Government: Lessons and Prospects for Iraq's Unstable Triangle*, Middle East Studies Occasional Papers, No. 2 (Quantico, VA: Marine Corps University Press, 2011).

10. Ibid.

11. Amit R. Paley, 'Shift in Tactics Aims to Revive Struggling Insurgency', *Washington Post*, 8 February 2008.

12. Ibid.

13. Andrew E. Kramer, 'U.S. Leaving Iraqi Comrades-in-Arms in Limbo', *New York Times*, 13 December 2011; Martin Chulov, 'Fears of al-Qaida Return in Iraq as US-Backed Fighters Defect', *Guardian*, 10 August 2010.

14. Marisa Cochrane Sullivan, 'Sunni Politicians Barred From Candidacy', Institute for the Study of War, 29 January 2010; Greg Caristrom, 'The Breakup: More Iraqis Bid for Autonomy', *Al Jazeera*, 22 December 2011.

15. Adam Strickland, 'Here is the Finalized OSC Translation of AQ Loyalist Abu Ahmad's Account of ISIL and its Origins', *Fund for Fallen Allies*, 25 September 2014, at: http://tinyurl.com/qa3eukq

16. English Translation of @Wikibaghdady, collected by Yousef Bin Tashfin, at: http://justpaste.it/e90q; 'The Islamic State of Iraq and Greater Syria: A Primer', *Soufan Group*, 13 June 2014; Bill Roggio, 'Al Qaeda Appoints New "War Minister" for Iraq', *Long War Journal*, 14 May 2010; Thomas Joscelyn, 'The Islamic State of Iraq and the Sham's Quiet War Minister', *Long War Journal*, 16 June 2014.

17. English Translation of @Wikibaghdady, collected by Yousef Bin Tashfin, at: http://justpaste.it/e90q

18. Ibid.; Bill Roggio, 'ISIS Confirms Death of Senior Leader in Syria', *Long War Journal*, 5 February 2014.

19. Michael Knights, 'The JRTN Movement and Iraq's Next Insurgency', Combating Terrorism Center at West Point, Vol. 4, No. 7, July 2011.

20. English Translation of @Wikibaghdady, collected by Yousef Bin Tashfin, at: http://justpaste.it/e90q

21. Bill Roggio, 'Al Qaeda in Iraq Claims Massacre at Christian Church in Baghdad', *Long War Journal*, 1 November 2010; Ernesto Londono, 'Survivors Describe Deadly Attack on Baghdad Church', *Washington Post*, 1 November 2010.

22. English Translation of @Wikibaghdady, collected by Yousef Bin Tashfin, at: http://justpaste.it/e90q; Noman Benotman and Roisin Blake, 'Jabhat al-Nusra: A Strategic Briefing', Quilliam Foundation, at: http://tinyurl.com/a7vcdmk

23. Thomas Joscelyn, 'Head of Al Nusrah Front Interviewed by Journalist Convicted in Spain on Controversial Terror Charges', *Long War Journal*, 13 December 2013; Pieter Van Ostaeyen, 'An Alleged Biography of Abu Muhammad al-Julani – Some Ideas', 16 December 2013, at: https://piet-ervanostaeyen.wordpress.com/

6. *Springtime for Qatar*

1. Nelly Lahoud with Muhammad al-'Ubaydi, 'Jihadi Discourse in the Wake of the Arab Spring', Harmony Program, Combating Terrorism Center at West Point, 17 December 2013.

2. Raphaël Lefèvre, 'The Syrian Brotherhood's Armed Struggle', Carnegie Endowment for International Peace, 14 December 2012; 'The Ubiquitous Arm of the Muslim Brotherhood?', *Syria Revolts*, 3 March 2012, at: https://syriarevolts.wordpress.com

3. Mary Beth Sheridan, 'U.S. to Expand Relations with Muslim Brotherhood', *Washington Post*, 30 June 2011; Christa Case Bryant, 'Behind Qatar's Bet on the Muslim Brotherhood', *Christian Science Monitor*, 18 April 2014.

4. Sultan Sooud al Qassemi, 'Qatar's Brotherhood Ties Alienate Fellow Gulf States', *Al-Monitor*, 23 January 2013.

5. Hugh Eakin, 'The Strange Power of Qatar', *New York Review of Books*, 27 October 2011.

6. Patrick E. Tyler, 'Intelligence Break Led U.S. to Tie Envoy Killing to Iraqi Qaeda Cell', *New York Times*, 6 February 2003; 'Al Qaeda Paymasters

"Living Freely" in Qatar', *Daily Star*, 18 November 2014; A. D. Kendall, '5 Qataris Who Fund Al Qaeda', *Money Jihad*, 30 June 2014, at: https://moneyjihad.wordpress.com; David D. Kirkpatrick, 'Qatar's Support of Islamists Alienates Near and Far', *New York Times*, 7 September 2014.

7. See press release, 'Boeing Delivers Qatar Emiri Air Force's 4th C-17 Globemaster III', Boeing, 10 December 2012; Hugh Naylor, 'Qatar's Single Border Crossing Exposes its Vulnerability', *The National*, 8 April 2014.

8. Judy Bachrach, 'WikiHistory: Did the Leaks Inspire the Arab Spring?' *World Affairs*, July–August 2011.

9. Andrew Hammond, 'Al Jazeera Loses Credibility for Censoring Coverage of Uprisings in Bahrain and Saudi Arabia, Acting as Propaganda Tool for Qatar's Role in Libya Intervention', *Peripheral Revision*, 14 April 2011, at: http://tinyurl.com/pfgapfn

10. 'Rafik Abdessalem', TunisiaLive at: www.tunisia-live.net/whoswho/rafik-abdessalem/; 'Rached Ghannouchi: «Le Qatar est un partenaire de la Révolution tunisienne»', 23 February 2012, at: www.youtube.com/watch?v=0lfPqjotgwI; Anna Mahjar-Barducci, 'Ruling Tunisia by Remote Control', *Haaretz*, 27 January 2012.

11. Steven Sotloff, 'Why the Libyans Have Fallen Out of Love with Qatar', *Time*, 2 January 2012; David Roberts. 'Behind Qatar's Intervention in Libya', *Foreign Affairs*, 28 September 2011; Ahmed Meiloud, 'Foreign Actors and the Libyan Civil War', *Middle East Eye*, 5 September 2014.

12. Sotloff, 'Why the Libyans Have Fallen Out of Love with Qatar'; Sam Dagher, Charles Levinson and Margaret Coker, 'Tiny Kingdom's Huge Role in Libya Draws Concern', *Wall Street Journal*, 17 October 2011.

7. The Road to Damascus

1. See Immam al-Albani, at: http://immamalbani.blogspot.de/2011/05/virtues-of-al-sham.html

2. Tina Rosenberg, 'Revolution U: What Egypt Learned from the Students who Overthrew Milosevic', *Foreign Policy*, 17 February 2011.

3. Joseph Holliday, 'The Struggle for Syria in 2011: An Operational and Regional Analysis', Institute for the Study of War, December 2011; 'Daraa: Ten Days of Massacres', International Federation for Human Rights, 5 May 2011.

4. Ian Black, 'Syrian Regime Document Trove Shows Evidence of "Industrial Scale" Killing of Detainees', *Guardian*, 21 January 2014; Ben

Hubbard and David D. Kirkpatrick, 'Photo Archive is Said to Show Widespread Torture in Syria', *New York Times*, 21 January 2014; 'A Report into the Credibility of Certain Evidence with Regard to Torture and Execution of Persons Incarcerated by the Current Syrian Regime', at: www.tagesschau.de/ausland/syrien3390.pdf

5. Mohammed Habash, 'Radical Are Assad's Best Friends', *The National*, 2 January 2014; Phil Sands, Justin Vela and Suha Maayeh, 'Assad Regime Set Free Extremists from Prison to Fire Up Trouble during Peaceful Uprising', *The National*, 21 January 2014.

6. 'Q&A: Nil Rosen on Syrian Sectarianism', *Al Jazeera*, 18 February 2012; Aron Lund, 'Who Are the Pro-Assad Militias?' Carnegie Endowment for International Peace, 2 March 2015.

7. Joseph Holliday, 'The Assad Regime: From Counterinsurgency to Civil War', Institute for the Study of War, March 2013.

8. 'Cracks in the Army: Defections from Bashar Assad's Armed Forces Are Growing', *The Economist*, 9 October 2011; Nada Bakri, 'Syrian Army Defectors Reportedly Kill 27 Soldiers', *New York Times*, 15 December 2011; Adam Entous and Joe Parkinson, 'Syrian Defectors Watch Civil War from the Sidelines', *Wall Street Journal*, 17 November 2014.

9. Joshua Landis, 'Western Press Misled – Who Shot the Nine Soldiers in Banyas? Not Syrian Security Forces', *Syria Comment*, 13 April 2011; Liam Stack and Katherine Zoepf, 'Syria Presses Crackdown in Two Cities on Coast', *New York Times*, 12 April 2011; Holliday, 'The Struggle for Syria in 2011'.

10. 'Syria Crisis: Investigating Jisr al-Shughour', BBC News, 22 June 2011; Andrea Glioti, 'Secrets of Jisr Al-Shughour: Was This Syria's Point of No Return?' *The Majalla*, 5 April 2012; Mariam Karouny, 'Syria to Send in Army after 120 Troops Killed', *Reuters*, 7 June 2011; Holliday, 'The Struggle for Syria in 2011'.

11. Roula Hajjar, 'Activist's Death Shocks Opposition', *Los Angeles Times*, 12 September 2011; Rania Abouzeid, 'U.S. to Syrians: "Don't Expect Another Libya"', *Time*, 28 September 2011.

12. 'Syria's Ramadan Massacre', *Washington Post*, 1 August 2011; Nada Bakri, 'Civilian Toll Is Mounting in Assault on Syrian City', *New York Times*, 4 August 2011.

13. Lt Col S. Edward Boxx, USAF, 'Observations on the Air War in Syria', *Air & Space Power Journal*, March–April 2013; Holliday, 'The Assad Regime'; 'Syria's Mutating Conflict', International Crisis Group, Middle East Report, No. 128, August 2012.

14. Robert Mood, 'My Experiences as Head of the UN Mission in Syria', Carnegie Endowment for International Peace, 21 January 2014.

15. Joshua Landis, 'Free Syrian Army Founded by Seven Officers to Fight the Syrian Army', *Syria Comment*, 29 July 2011; Local Coordinating Committees in Syria, 'Syrian Local Coordinating Committees on Taking Up Arms and Foreign Intervention', Facebook page, 29 August 2011.

8. *Prince Bandar's Last Adventure*

1. Ken Sofer and Juliana Shafroth, 'The Structure and Organization of the Syrian Opposition', Center for American Progress, 14 May 2013.

2. Sibel Edmonds, 'Secret US–NATO Training & Support Camp to Oust Current Syrian President', *Boiling Frogs Post*, 21 November 2011, at: http://tinyurl.com/78ylsr4

3. C. J. Chivers, 'How to Control Libya Missiles? Buy Them Up', *New York Times*, 22 December 2011; 'US State Department Public Accountability Board Report', 18 December 2013, at: www.state.gov/documents/organization/202446.pdf

4. Asher Berman, 'Rebel Groups in Jebel al-Zawiyah', Institute for the Study of War, 26 July 2012; Joseph Holliday, 'The Struggle for Syria in 2011: An Operational and Regional Analysis', Institute for the Study of War, December 2011.

5. 'Treasury Designates Al-Qa'ida Supporters in Qatar and Yemen', U.S. Department of the Treasury, 18 December 2013, at: www.treasury.gov/press-center/press-releases/Pages/jl2249.aspx; David Andrew Weinberg, 'Qatar and Terror Finance', Foundation for Defense of Democracies, 10 December 2014; Roula Khalaf and Abigail Fielding-Smith, 'How Qatar Seized Control of the Syrian Revolution', *Financial Times*, 17 May 2013.

6. Elizabeth Dickinson, 'Playing with Fire: Why Private Gulf Financing for Syria's Extremist Rebels Risks Igniting Sectarian Conflict at Home', Brookings Institution, No. 16, December 2013; Elizabeth Dickinson, 'Kuwait, "The Back Office of Logistical Support" for Syria's Rebels', *The National*, 5 February 2013; Karen DeYoung, 'Kuwait, Ally on Syria, is Also the Leading Funder of Extremist Rebels', *Washington Post*, 25 April 2014; 'Remarks of Under Secretary for Terrorism and Financial Intelligence David Cohen before the Center for a New American Security on "Confronting New Threats in Terrorist Financing"', U.S. Department of the Treasury, 4 March 2014.

7. Asher Berman, 'Rebel Financiers Flock to Northern Syria', Syria Survey, 30 June 2013; 'You Can Still See Their Blood', Human Rights Watch, 10 October 2013.

8. 'Syria Says Twin Suicide Bombs in Damascus Kill 44', BBC News, 23 December 2011; Bill Rogio, 'Al Nusrah Front Launches Complex Suicide Assault on Syrian Air Force Intelligence HQ', *Long War Journal*, 9 October 2012.

9. Mark Hosenball, 'Obama Authorizes Secret Support for Syrian Rebels', *Reuters*, 1 August 2012.

10. Karen DeYoung and Liz Sly, 'Syrian Rebels get Influx of Arms with Gulf Neighbors' Money, U.S. Coordination', *Washington Post*, 15 May 2012; C. J. Chivers and Eric Schmitt, 'Arms Airlift to Syria Rebels Expands, With Aid From C.I.A.', *New York Times*, 24 March 2013.

11. Fielding-Smith, 'How Qatar Seized Control of the Syrian Revolution'; David E. Sanger, 'Rebel Arms Flow is Said to Benefit Jihadists in Syria', *New York Times*, 14 October 2012; Blake Hounshell, 'Iraq Accuses Qatar of Financing Jihadi Groups in Syria', *Foreign Policy*, 4 March 2013.

12. 'Final Report of the Panel of Experts Established Pursuant to Resolution 1973 (2011) Concerning Libya', United Nations Security Council, 15 February 2014, at: www.un.org/ga/search/view_doc. asp?symbol=S/2014/106; Jane Mayer, 'The C.I.A.'s Travel Agent', *New Yorker*, 30 October 2006.

13. Letter dated 15 February 2013 from the Panel of Experts on Libya Established Pursuant to Resolution 1973 (2011), United Nations Security Council, www.un.org/ga/search/view_doc.asp?symbol=S/2013/99; Rania Abouzeid, 'Arming Syria's Rebellion: How Libyan Weapons and Know-How Reach Anti-Assad Fighters', *Time*, 29 May 2013.

14. Frederic Wehrey, 'Saudi Arabia Reins In Its Clerics on Syria', Carnegie Endowment for International Peace, 14 June 2012; Hassan Hassan, 'Saudis Overtaking Qatar in Sponsoring Syrian Rebels', *The National*, 15 May 2013.

15. Adam Entous, Nour Malas and Margaret Coker, 'A Veteran Saudi Power Player Works to Build Support to Topple Assad', *Wall Street Journal*, 25 August 2013.

16. Phil Sands and Suha Maayeh, 'Syrian Rebels Get Arms and Advice through Secret Command Centre in Amman', *The National*, 28 December 2013.

17. C. J. Chivers and Eric Schmitt, 'Saudis Step Up Help for Rebels in Syria with Croatian Arms', *New York Times*, 25 February 2013; Rania Abouzeid, 'Syria's Secular and Islamist Rebels: Who Are the Saudis and

Qataris Arming?', *Time*, 18 September 2012 ; Richard Spencer, 'US and Europe in "Major Airlift of Arms to Syrian Rebels through Zagreb"', *Daily Telegraph*, 8 March 2013.

18. Geoff Dyer, 'US Urges Change in Syrian Rebels' Leaders', *Financial Times*, 31 October 2012; Hassan, 'Saudis Overtaking Qatar in Sponsoring Syrian Rebels'; Mohammad Ballout, 'Syrian Opposition Attempts Consolidation', *Al-Monitor*, 11 May 2013.

19. 'Qatar Readies for Leadership Shuffle as PM Prepares to Step Down', *Daily Star*, 17 June 2013; Mohammad Ballout, 'Will Qatar's Emir Abdicate in August?' *Al-Monitor*, 11 June 2013.

20. Hassan, 'Saudis Overtaking Qatar in Sponsoring Syrian Rebels'.

9. Knights of the Silencers

1. 'Gunmen in Iraq Take Over Bus Filled with Shiite Pilgrims and Kill 22 Men', *New York Times*, 12 September 2011.

2. Juan Cole, 'Iraq's al-Maliki Seeks Arrest of Sunni VP as Terrorist, Parliament in Uproar', 18 December 2011, at: http://tinyurl.com/ccosfuf

3. Marisa Sullivan, 'Maliki's Authoritarian Rule', Institute for the Study of War, April 2013.

4. 'Country Reports on Human Rights Practices for 2012', US Department of State, at: www.state.gov/j/drl/rls/hrrpt/2012humanrightsreport/; 'Iraq Protesters Win First Demand: Release of 3,000 Prisoners', *Middle East Online*, 3 February 2013.

5. Jim Loney, 'Are the Iraqi Security Forces Ready or Not?' *Reuters*, 12 August 2010; Martin Chulov, 'Saddam Hussein Deputy Tariq Aziz Calls for US Forces to Stay in Iraq', *Guardian*, 5 August 2010; Michael Knights, 'The Iraqi Security Forces: Local Context and U.S. Assistance', Washington Institute for Near East Policy, June 2011.

6. Ramzy Mardini, 'Iraq's Post-Withdrawal Crisis, Update 1, December 15–19, 2011', Institute for the Study of War, 19 December 2011; Ramzy Mardini, 'Iraq's Recurring Political Crisis', Institute for the Study of War, 16 February 2012; Stephen Wicken, 'The Hashemi Verdict and the Health of Democracy in Iraq', Institute for the Study of War, 11 September 2012; 'Iraq: Mass Arrests, Incommunicado Detentions', Human Rights Watch, 15 May 2012.

7. Michael S. Schmidt and Eric Schmitt, 'Leaving Iraq, U.S. Fears New Surge of Qaeda Terror', *New York Times,* 5 November 2011; Nawzat

Shamdeen, 'Al-Qaeda's Secrets: The Protection Money Racket in Mosul – 2910', *Niqash*, 17 January 2012; Harith al-Qarawee, 'Al-Qaeda Sinks Roots in Mosul, *Al-Monitor*, 24 October 2013.

8. Pieter Van Ostaeyen, 'The Iraqi Prison Break: A Viewpoint', 22 July 2012, at: https://pietervanostaeyen.wordpress.com

9. Aki Peritz, 'The Great Iraqi Jail Break', *Foreign Policy*, 26 June 2014.

10. Anthony H. Cordesman, 'Violence in Iraq: The Growing Risk of Serious Civil Conflict', Center for Strategic and International Studies, 9 September 2013.

11. 'Stormings Are More Painful' English translation of speech of Sheikh Abu Mohammad al-Adnani, Al-Furqan Media, 12 November 2012, at: http://tinyurl.com/pw4ygwc; Bill Ardolino, 'Al Qaeda in Iraq Video Shows Series of Attacks Against Iraqi Security Forces', *Long War Journal*, 26 January 2013.

12. 'Iraq's Sunni Finance Minister Denounces Raids', BBC, 21 December 2012.

13. Yasir Ghazi and Christine Hauser, 'Iraq's Sadr Encourages Antigovernment Demonstrations', *New York Times*, 1 January 2013; Sam Wyer, 'Political Update: Mapping the Iraq Protests', Institute for the Study of War, 11 January 2013; Sam Dagher, 'Saddam's Brethren Get Organized', *Wall Street Journal*, 11 April 2013.

14. 'Iraq after Hawija: Recovery or Relapse', International Crisis Group, 26 April 2013; 'Iraq: Falluja's Faustian Bargain', International Crisis Group, 28 April 2014.

15. Matt Bradley and Ali A. Nabhan, 'Iraq Raids Protesters Camp', *Wall Street Journal*, 23 April 2013.

16. Marah Mashi, 'ISIS Threatens Ismaili Capital of Syria', *Al Akhbar*, 30 October 2014.

17. Cordesman, 'Violence in Iraq'.

18. Marisa Cochrane Sullivan, '2013 Iraq Update #17B: Iraq on the Edge', Institute for the Study of War, 28 April 2013; Nabhan, 'Iraq Raids Protesters Camp'; 'Iraq: Fallujah's Faustian Bargain'; Jessica Lewis and ISW Iraq Team, 'Iraqi Update 2014 #1: Showdown in Anbar', Institute for the Study of War, 3 January 2014.

19. Bill Roggio, 'Al Qaeda, Tribal Allies "Control" Fallujah', *Long War Journal*, 4 January 2014; Liz Sly, 'Al-Qaeda Force Captures Fallujah Amid Rise in Violence in Iraq', *Washington Post*, 3 January 2014.

10. *Treasure of Babisqa*

1. Rania Abouzeid, 'Syria's Up-and-Coming Rebels: Who Are the Farouq Brigades?' *Time*, 5 October 2012.
2. Lucas Winter, 'Raqqa: From Regime Overthrow to Inter-Rebel Fighting', Foreign Military Studies Office, March 2014, at: http://fmso.leavenworth. army.mil/documents/Raqqa.pdf
3. Avi Melamed, 'A Disturbing Scenario in the Golan Heights', 20 September 2012, at: https://avimelamed.com/2012/09/21/a-disturbing-scenario-in-the-golan-heights/; Khaled Yacoub Oweis, 'Turf War Feared after Syrian Rebel Leader Killed', *Reuters*, 11 January 2013.
4. Nour Malas, 'As Syrian Islamists Gain, It's Rebel Against Rebel', *Wall Street Journal*, 29 May 2013.
5. Adam Brodie, 'The al-Absi Brothers – ISIS Precursor in Aleppo', November 2014, at: https://storify.com/AdamBrodie1/the-al-absi-brothers-isis-precursor-in-aleppo; English Translation of @Wikibaghdady, collected by Yousef Bin Tashfin, at: http://justpaste.it/e90q
6. Brodie, 'The al-Absi Brothers – ISIS precursor in Aleppo'; Winter, 'Raqqa: From Regime Overthrow to Inter-Rebel Fighting'; The Soufan Group, 'ISIS Leadership', *Frontline*, at: http://apps.frontline.org/isis-leadership/
7. Aron Lund, 'Showdown at Bab al-Hawa', Carnegie Endowment for International Peace, 12 December 2013.
8. David Ignatius, 'Al-Qaeda Affiliate Playing Larger Role in Syria Rebellion', *Washington Post*, 30 November 2012; Bill Roggio and Thomas Joscelyn, 'Zarqawi's Brother-in-Law Reported Killed While Leading Al Nusra Front Unit', *Long War Journal*, 14 December 2012.
9. Bill Roggio, 'Al Nusrah Front Commanded Free Syrian Army Unit, "Chechen Emigrants", in Assault on Syrian Air Defense Base', *Long War Journal*, 19 October 2012.
10. David Butter, 'Fueling Conflict: Syria's War for Oil and Gas', Carnegie Endowment for International Peace, 2 April 2014; Matthew Barber and the Syria Video Team, 'Oil Wars – Nusra's Expanding Reach – Syrian Taliban', Syria Comment, 27 April 2013, at: www.joshualandis.com/ blog/oil-wars-nusras-expanding-reach-syrian-taliban/
11. Lucas Winter, 'Raqqa: From Regime Overthrow to Inter-Rebel Fighting', Foreign Military Studies Office, March 2014, at: http://fmso. leavenworth.army.mil/documents/Raqqa.pdf; Bill Roggio, 'Syrian Jihadists, Including Al Qaeda's Al Nusrah Front, Form Mujahideen

Shura Council', *Long War Journal*, 12 December 2012; Bill Roggio, 'Al Nusrah Front Spearheads Capture of Syrian Dam, Claims Suicide Assault', *Long War Journal*, 11 February 2013.

12. Malas, 'As Syrian Islamists Gain, It's Rebel Against Rebel'.
13. Joseph Holliday, 'The Opposition Takeover in Al-Raqqa', Institute for the Study of War, 15 March 2013.
14. Ibid.
15. Firas al-Hakkar, 'The Mysterious Fall of Raqqa, Syria's Kandahar', *Al-Akhbar*, 8 November 2013; Winter, 'Raqqa: From Regime Overthrow to Inter-Rebel Fighting'.
16. 'How did Raqqa Fall to the Islamic State of Iraq and Syria?' *Syria Untold*, 13 January 2014, at: http://tinyurl.com/p6n3aka
17. Rania Abouzeid, 'How Islamist Rebels in Syria Are Ruling a Fallen Provincial Capital', *Time*, 23 March 2013.

11. Chain of Custody

1. Bill Roggio, 'Syrian Government Accuses Rebels of Launching Chemical Attack', *Long War Journal*, 19 March 2013.
2. Bill Roggio, 'Al Nusrah Front, Foreign Jihadists Seize Key Syrian Base in Aleppo', *Long War Journal*, 10 December 2012; 'Rebels Could Resort to Chemical Weapons, Syria Warns', France24, 8 December 2012.
3. Kim Willsher, 'Syria Crisis: French Intelligence Dossier Blames Assad for Chemical Attack', *Guardian*, 2 September 2013.
4. Basma Atassi, 'Insider Sheds Light on Syria's Chemical Arms', *Al Jazeera*, 23 May 2013.
5. Ronen Bergman, Juliane von Mittelstaedt, Matthias Schepp and Holger Stark, 'Israel's Red Line: Fate of Syrian Chemical Weapons may Trigger War', *Spiegel Online*, 31 July 2012.
6. 'Remarks by the President to the White House Press Corps', 20 August 2012, at: www.whitehouse.gov/the-press-office/2012/08/20/remarks-president-white-house-press-corps
7. Atassi, 'Insider Sheds Light on Syria's Chemical Arms'.
8. Jean-Philippe Rémy, 'Chemical Warfare in Syria', *Le Monde*, 27 May 2013.
9. Rémy, 'Chemical Warfare in Syria'; 'Attacks on Ghouta: Analysis of Alleged Use of Chemical Weapons in Syria', Human Rights Watch, 10 September 2013.

10. 'Syria: Reported Chemical Weapons Use', Letter from Chairman of the Joint Intelligence Committee, 29 August 2013; Jonathon Burch, 'Turkey Arrests 12 in Raids on "Terrorist" Organization', *Reuters*, 30 May 2013.

11. Mary Beth D. Nikitin, Paul K. Kerr and Andrew Feickert, 'Syria's Chemical Weapons: Issues for Congress', Congressional Research Service, 30 September 2013.

12. Matthew Weaver and Brian Whitaker, 'Syria Crisis: UN Mission Given 30 Day Extension – Friday 20 July 2012', *Guardian*, 20 July 2012.

13. Bill Roggio, 'Iraq Attacks and the Syrian Connection', *Long War Journal*, 30 August 2009; 'From The UN Report', *Reuters*, 22 October 2005, see www.washingtonpost.com/wp-dyn/content/article/2005/10/21/AR2005102102212.html

14. Valerie Szybala, 'Assad Strikes Damascus: The Battle for Syria's Capital', Institute for the Study of War, January 2014.

15. Sammy Ketz, 'Under Damascus, Rebels and Army Battle in Maze of Tunnels', *Times of Israel*, 6 June 2014.

16. Elizabeth O'Bagy, 'The Opposition Advances in Damascus', Institute for the Study of War, 9 August 2013; Martin Chulov and Harriet Sherwood, 'Syrian Troop Redeployments Raise Concerns over Golan Heights Security', *Guardian*, 7 April 2013; Szybala, 'Assad Strikes Damascus: The Battle for Syria's Capital'; Edith M. Lederer, 'Death Toll In Syria Rises To 100,000, UN Chief Ban Ki-Moon Says', Associated Press, 25 July 2013.

17. 'Attacks on Ghouta: Analysis of Alleged Use of Chemical Weapons in Syria'.

18. 'The Alleged Chemical Attack Sites in Damascus', *Washington Post*, 30 August 2013.

19. See Press Release, 'Syria: Thousands Suffering from Neurotoxic Symptoms Treated in Hospitals Supported by MSF', Médecins Sans Frontières, 24 August 2013; Nikitin, Kerr and Feickert, 'Syria's Chemical Weapons: Issues for Congress'.

20. 'Israel TV: Chemical Weapons were Fired by Assad's Brother's Unit', *Times of Israel*, 24 August 2013.

21. Seymour M. Hersh, 'The Red Line and the Rat Line', *London Review of Books*, Vol. 36, No. 8, 17 April 2014; Eliot Higgins and Dan Kaszeta, 'It's Clear that Turkey was Not Involved in the Chemical Attack on Syria', *Guardian*, 22 April 2014.

22. Vladimir V. Putin, 'A Plea for Caution from Russia', *New York Times*, 11 September 2013.

23. 'Turkey is Not Like Egypt', BBC Turkish, 23 August 2013.

24. 'Public Opinion Drove Syria Debate', YouGov, 30 August 2013, at: https://yougov.co.uk/news/2013/08/30/public-opinion-syria-policy/; Scott Clement, 'Most in U.S. Oppose Syria Strike, Post-ABC Poll Finds', *Washington Post*, 3 September 2013.

25. Hersh, 'The Red Line and the Rat Line'; Thom Shanker, C. J. Chivers and Michael R. Gordon, 'Obama Weighs "Limited" Strikes Against Syrian Forces', *New York Times*, 27 August 2013.

26. Khaled Yacoub Oweis, 'Syrian Army Moves Scud Missiles to Avoid Strike', *Reuters*, 29 August 2013; Szybala, 'Assad Strikes Damascus: The Battle for Syria's Capital'.

27. Conal Urquhart, 'Syria Crisis: US and Russia Agree Chemical Weapons Deal', *Guardian*, 14 September 2013.

28. Nour Malas, 'Syrian Rebels Hurt By Delay', *Wall Street Journal*, 11 September 2013.

12. Game of Thrones

1. Giles Tremlett, 'When a Reporter Got too Close to the Story', *Guardian*, 3 October 2005; 'Al-Qaeda leader in Syria Speaks to Al Jazeera', *Al Jazeera*, 19 December 2013.

2. Bill Roggio, 'Abu Musab al Suri Released from Syrian Custody: Report', *Long War Journal*, 6 February 2012; Aron Lund, 'Who and What was Abu Khaled al-Suri? Part II', Carnegie Endowment for International Peace, 25 February 2014.

3. Brynjar Lia, *Architect of Global Jihad: The Life of Al-Qaida Strategist Abu Mus'ab Al-Suri* (New York: Columbia University Press, 2008); David Samuels, 'The New Mastermind of Jihad', *Wall Street Journal*, 6 April 2012.

4. Steven Stalinsky, 'Al-Qaeda Military Strategist Abu Mus'ab Al-Suri's Teachings on Fourth-Generation Warfare (4GW), Individual Jihad and the Future of Al-Qaeda', Middle East Media Research Institute (MEMRI), 22 June 2011; Hassan Hassan, 'A Jihadist Blueprint for Hearts and Minds is Gaining Traction in Syria', *The National*, 4 March 2014.

5. Ghaith Abdul-Ahad, 'Syria's Nusra Front – Ruthless, Organised and Taking Control', *Guardian*, 10 July 2013.

6. Aymenn Jawad Al-Tamimi, 'The Islamic State of Iraq and al-Sham', *Middle East Review of International Affairs* (MERIA), Vol. 17, No. 3 (Fall 2013).

7. Ibid.

8. Hamza al-Mustapha, 'Al Nusra Front: From Formation to Dissension', Arab Center for Research and Policy Studies, February 2014.

9. Abdul-Ahad, 'Syria's Nusra Front – Ruthless, Organised and Taking Control'.

10. English Translation of @Wikibaghdady, collected by Yousef Bin Tashfin, at: http://justpaste.it/e90

11. Thomas Joscelyn, 'Analysis: Zawahiri's Letter to Al Qaeda Branches in Syria, Iraq', *Long War Journal*, 10 June 2013.

12. Cole Bunzel, 'The Islamic State of Disobedience: al-Baghdadi Triumphant', *Jihadica*, 5 October 2013, at: www.jihadica.com

13. Mariam Karouny, 'Insight: Syria's Nusra Front Eclipsed by Iraq-Based al Qaeda', *Reuters*, 17 May 2013.

14. Suhaib Anjarini, 'The Evolution of ISIS', *Al-Monitor*, 1 November 2013.

15. @Wikibaghdady, at: http://justpaste.it/e90; Thomas Joscelyn, 'Chechen-Led Group Swears Allegiance to Head of Islamic State of Iraq and Sham', *Long War Journal*, 27 November 2013.

16. Valerie Szybala, 'Al Qaeda Shows its True Colours in Syria', Institute for the Study of War, 1 August 2013; Aymenn Jawad al-Tamimi, 'Where Does Jabhat al-Nusra End, and the Islamic State of Iraq & Ash-Sham Begin?' *Syria Comment*, 13 July 2013; 'Syria: Countrywide Conflict Report #4', Carter Center, 11 September 2014.

17. Szybala, 'Al Qaeda Shows Its True Colours in Syria'.

18. Valerie Szybala, 'The Islamic Alliance Emerges', Institute for the Study of War, 27 September 2013; Lisa Lundquist, 'Formation of Islamic Front in Syria Benefits Jihadist Groups', *Long War Journal*, 23 November 2013.

19. Bill Roggio, 'Free Syrian Army Brigades Join Al Nusra Front', *Long War Journal*, 20 September 2013; Bill Roggio, 'Free Syrian Army Units Ally with Al Qaeda, Reject Syrian National Coalition, and Call for Sharia', *Long War Journal*, 26 September 2013; Bill Roggio, 'Free Syrian Army Continues to Fracture as More Units Defect', *Long War Journal*, 17 October 2013.

20. Joshua Landis, 'The Battle Between ISIS and Syria's Rebel Militias', Syria Comment, 4 January 2014.

21. Marlin Dick, 'FSA Alliance Pushes Back Against Islamic Front', *Daily Star*, 17 December 2013; Lisa Lundquist, 'Islamic Front Fighters Take Over Free Syrian Army Bases Near Turkish Border', *Long War Journal*, 7 December 2013; 'Free Syrian Army Fires Military Chief', *Al Jazeera*, 18 February 2014.

22. 'More Than 50 Executed in Aleppo Bloodbath as Rebels Turn Against Each Other', *Daily Mail*, 8 January 2014.

23. 'Citizen Journalist in Aleppo: ISIS "Treated Us Worse Than Air Force Intelligence"', *Syria: Direct*, 8 January 2014; Jeralyn, 'Theo Padnos' Remarkable Account of Captivity and Torture', 31 October 2014, at: www.talkleft.com

24. Nelly Lahoud and Muhammad al-'Ubaydi, 'The War of Jihadists Against Jihadists in Syria', Combating Terrorism Center, 26 March 2014.

25. Radwan Mortada, 'Syria: Al Nusra Front Declares War on ISIS', *Al-Akhbar*, 26 February 2014.

13. Paradise Square

1. Lucas Winter, 'Raqqa: From Regime Overthrow to Inter-Rebel Fighting', Foreign Military Studies Office, March 2014; Charles C. Caris and Samuel Reynolds, 'ISIS Governance in Syria', Institute for the Study of War, July 2014.

2. Pieter Van Ostaeyen, 'The Ar-Raqqa Executions', 15 May 2013, at: https://pietervanostaeyen.wordpress.com

3. Scott Lucas, 'Syria Special: What is Life Like in Raqqa under Islamic State of Iraq?' EA WorldView, 9 June 2014; Anon, 'The Last Alawite in Raqqa', *London Review of Books*, 2 August 2013; 'Rule of Terror: Living under ISIS in Syria', Report of the Independent Commission of Inquiry on the Syrian Arab Republic, 14 November 2014.

4. Alison Tahmizian Meuse, 'In Raqqa, Islamist Rebels Form a New Regime', Syria Deeply, 16 August 2013; Francesca Paci, 'Still No News of Kidnapped Jesuit Priest, Fr. Dall'Oglio, after Five Months of Silence', *Vatican Insider*, 29 December 2013.

5. Caris and Reynolds, 'ISIS Governance in Syria'.

6. Mona Mahmood, 'Double-layered Veils and Despair ... Women Describe Life under ISIS', *Guardian*, 17 February 2015; Abu Ibrahim al-Raqqawi, 'Inside the Islamic State "Capital": No End in Sight to its Grim Rule', *Guardian*, 21 February 2015.

7. 'ISIS Establishes Itself in Eastern and Northern Syria', Crethiplethi, 22 May 2015, at: www.crethiplethi.com

8. Lydia Smith, 'Islamic State's Women Warriors: How Feared Al-Khansa Battalion was Borne Out of Repression', *International Business Times*, 13 August 2014.

9. Jamie Dettmer, 'Bloodshed, Indoctrination Mark Islamic Militants' Rule in Raqqa', *Voice of America*, 17 January 2015.

10. 'As Jihadist Rebels Burn Two Catholic Churches in ar-Raqqah, Assad's Enemies Openly Split', *AsiaNews*, 27 September 2013.

11. 'ISIS Closes Schools in Syria, Leaving 670,000 Children without Education', Reuters, 6 January 2015; Megan Specia, 'ISIS Reportedly Recruits Children through "Cub Camps"', Mashable, 7 November 2014.

12. 'The Raqqa Woman who Faced the Islamic State of Iraq and Syria', Syria Untold, 17 October 2013; 'Activists in Raqqa Face Deadly Threats', *Syrian Observer*, 10 December 2013.

13. Mark Townsend, 'Inside the Islamic State's Capital: Red Bull-Drinking Jihadists, Hungry Civilians, Crucifixions and Air Strikes', *Guardian*, 30 November 2014; Ali Hashem, 'Life in Raqqa under IS', *Al-Monitor*, 3 November 2014; Ruth Sherlock and Carol Malouf, 'Inside an ISIL Town: "Raqqa is Being Slaughtered Silently"', *Daily Telegraph*, 23 August 2014.

14. Jacob Siegel, 'Islamic Extremists Now Crucifying People in Syria – And Tweeting Out the Pictures', *Daily Beast*, 30 April 2014; Raslan Trad, 'An Interview with One Syrian Activist in Raqqa Who Is Fighting Bashar al-Assad and ISIS', *Muftah*, 8 January 2015.

15. Liz Sly, 'The Islamic State is Failing at Being a State', *Washington Post*, 25 December 2014.

16. Aaron Zelin, 'The Islamic State of Iraq and Syria has a Consumer Protection Office', *The Atlantic*, 13 June 2014; Mariam Karouny, 'Life under ISIS: For Residents of Raqqa is This Really a Caliphate Worse Than Death?' *The Independent*, 5 September 2014.

17. Damien Gayle, 'Women Stoned to Death in Syria for Adultery', *Associated Press*, 9 August 2014.

14. Birth of a Nation

1. Charles C. Caris and Samuel Reynolds, 'ISIS Governance in Syria', Institute for the Study of War, July 2014; 'Syria Countrywide Conflict Report # 4', Carter Center, 11 September 2014.

2. Bill Roggio, 'ISIS Confirms Death of Senior Leader in Syria', *Long War Journal*, 5 February 2014; Caris and Reynolds, 'ISIS Governance in Syria'; Mitchell Prothero, 'Al Qaida's ISIS Takes 2 Syrian Cities, Executes Scores of Rivals', McClatchy, 13 January 2014.

3. Aymenn Jawad Al-Tamimi, 'The Factions of Abu Khamal', *Middle East Forum*, 18 December 2013; Mariam Karouny, 'In Eastern Syria, Oil

Smugglers Benefit from Chaos', *Reuters*, 9 May 2013; Hassan Hassan, 'Lessons for Syria's Future from Jihadi Infighting in Deir Ezzor', *The National*, 11 February 2014; Bill Roggio, 'Islamic State Consolidates Gains in Eastern Syria', *Long War Journal*, 3 July 2014.

4. Caris and Reynolds, 'ISIS Governance in Syria'.

5. Prothero, 'Al Qaida's ISIS Takes 2 Syrian Cities, Executes Scores of Rivals'; 'Syria Countrywide Conflict Report # 4'; Caris and Reynolds, 'ISIS Governance in Syria'.

6. Valerie Szybala, 'The Islamic State of Iraq and al-Sham and the "Cleansing" of Deir ez-Zour', Institute for the Study of War, 14 May 2014; 'Syria Countrywide Conflict Report # 4'; Deborah Haynes and Laura Pitel, 'FSA Strikes Jihadist-Held Stronghold', *The Times*, 26 April 2014; 'Al Qaeda Offshoot in Fierce Offensive, Carves Out Territory Across Syria and Iraq', *Reuters*, 10 June 2014.

7. 'Islamic State Expels Rivals from Syrian City', *Al Jazeera*, 15 July 2014.

8. 'Iraq: Falluja's Faustian Bargain', International Crisis Group, 28 April 2014; Juan Cole, 'Iraq's Sunni Civil War', 4 January 2014, at: www.juancole.com

9. 'Iraq: Falluja's Faustian Bargain'.

10. Arthur Bright, 'John Kerry on Iraq's Growing Al Qaeda Problem: "This is their Fight"', *Christian Science Monitor*, 6 January 2014; Josh Rogin, 'Congress to Iraq's Maliki: No Arms for a Civil War', *Daily Beast*, 8 January 2014.

11. 'Iraq: Bringing Urgently Needed Help to Civilians in Fallujah', International Committee of the Red Cross, 28 January 2014; 'UN: Clashes in Iraq's Anbar Displaced 300,000', *Al Jazeera*, 12 February 2014.

12. 'Iraq Army Using "Barrel Bombs" in Fallujah', *Al Jazeera*, 11 May 2014; Patrick Cockburn, 'The Battle for Fallujah: Fighting Returns to Iraqi City as al-Qa'ida-Linked Rebels Gain Stronghold', *Independent*, 18 May 2014.

13. Daniel Pipes, 'The Acute Danger of Iraqi Dams', *National Review Online*, 1 July 2014; Jessica Lewis, 'ISIS Besieged Areas Near Baghdad on Eve of Elections', Institute for the Study of War, 25 April 2014.

14. Sinan Adnan with Aaron Reese, 'Beyond the Islamic State: Iraq's Sunni Insurgency', Institute for the Study of War, October 2014; Joel Wing, 'Precarious Relationship Between the Islamic State of Iraq and the Baathist Naqshibandi', *Musings on Iraq*, 25 June 2014.

15. Martin Chulov, 'ISIS insurgents seize control of Iraqi city of Mosul', *The Guardian*, 10 June 2014; Ned Parker, Isabel Coles and Raheem Salman,

'Special Report: How Mosul Fell – An Iraqi General Disputes Baghdad's Story', *Reuters*, 14 October 2014; Michael Pregent and Michael Weiss, 'Exploiting the ISIS Vulnerabilities in Iraq', *Wall Street Journal*, 12 August 2014.

16. Jessica Lewis, 'The Islamic State of Iraq and Al-Sham Captures Mosul and Advances Towards Baghdad', Institute for the Study of War, 11 June 2014; Suadad al-Salhy and Tim Arango, 'Iraq Militants, Pushing South, Aim at Capital', *New York Times*, 11 June 2014; Debra Heine, 'What Happened at the Camp Speicher Massacre in Iraq?' Breitbart, 4 September 2014; 'Iraq: Islamic State Executions in Tikrit', Human Rights Watch, 2 September 2014.

17. 'Iraq: ISIS Executed Hundreds of Prison Inmates', Human Rights Watch, 30 October 2014.

15. Twitter Caliphate

1. Aron Lund, 'Reporting Syria: An Interview With Rania Abouzeid', Carnegie Endowment for International Peace, 26 November 2013.

2. Paul Wood, 'In Syria, Facing Danger From All Sides', Committee to Protect Journalists, February 2013; Kim Sengupta, 'Two Terror Suspects Arrested at Heathrow Airport in the First Case of the Syrian Civil War Leading to the Arrest of Suspected Terrorists in the UK', *Independent*, 10 October 2012.

3. John Cantlie, 'Hard Talk: The Real Story Behind My Videos', *Dabiq*, No. 4, at: http://tinyurl.com/mtddsb6

4. James Traub, 'The Disappeared', *Foreign Policy*, 22 January 2014.

5. 'Journalism in Syria: Impossible Job?' Reporters Without Borders, 6 November 2013; 'Rule of Terror: Living under ISIS in Syria', UN Report of the Independent International Commission of Inquiry in the Syrian Arab Republic, 14 November 2014.

6. Bill Ardolino and Bill Roggio,'Al Qaeda in Iraq Video Details Deadly Raid in Haditha', *Long War Journal*, 21 August 2012; Bill Ardolino, 'Al Qaeda in Iraq Video Shows Series of Attacks Against Iraqi Security Forces', *Long War Journal*, 26 January 2013.

7. Bryan Price, Dan Milton and Muhammad al-'Ubaydi, 'CTC Perspectives: Al-Baghdadi's Blitzkreig, ISIL's Psychological Warfare, and What It Means for Syria and Iraq', Combating Terrorism Center at West Point, 12 June 2014.

8. James Cook, 'Third Jihadist in Isis Video is from Aberdeen', BBC News, 24 June 2014.

9. *Dabiq*, No. 3, at: http://media.clarionproject.org

10. Souad Mekhennet and Adam Goldman, '"Jihadi John": Islamic State Killer is Identified as Londoner Mohammed Emwazi', *Washington Post*, 26 February 2015.

11. Cantlie, 'Hard Talk: The Real Story Behind my Videos'.

12. Ibid.

13. J. Klausen, 'Tweeting the Jihad: Social Media Networks of Western Foreign Fighters in Syria and Iraq', *Studies in Conflict and Terrorism*, 38:1, 9 December 2014.

14. J. M. Berger, 'How ISIS Games Twitter', *The Atlantic*, 16 June 2014; Faisal Irshaid, 'How ISIS is Spreading its Message Online', BBC News, 19 June 2014; James P. Farwell, 'How ISIS Uses Social Media', International Institute for Strategic Studies, 2 October 2014; Cahal Milmo, 'ISIS Jihadists Using World Cup and Premier League Hashtags to Promote Extremist Propaganda on Twitter', *Independent*, 22 June 2014.

15. Lauren Walker, 'Inside the ISIS Social Media Campaign', *Newsweek*, 6 March 2015.

16. *Call of Duty*

1. 'ISIS Abu Bakr al-Baghdadi First Friday Sermon as So-Called "Caliph"', *Al Arabiya*, 5 July 2014.

2. 'ISIS Captures Iraq–Syria Border Post', *Al-Akhbar*, 21 June 2014.

3. 'Report on the Protection of Civilians in the Non International Armed Conflict in Iraq: 5 June–5 July 2014', United Nations Assistance Mission for Iraq (UNAMI)/Office of the High Commissioner for Human Rights, http://tinyurl.com/qjpyxn3; Dalshad Abdullah, 'Two Million Iraqi Refugees in Kurdistan: Official', *Asharq al-Awsat*, 27 December 2014.

4. 'In New Message Following Being Declared A "Caliph," Islamic State Leader Abu Bakr Al-Baghdadi Promises Support To Oppressed Muslims Everywhere, Tells His Soldiers: "You Will Conquer Rome"', *MEMRI: Jihad and Terrorism Threat Monitor*, 1 July 2014, at: http://tinyurl.com/qfvcwsh

5. Sheikh Abu Turki bin Mubarek al-Benali, 'A Biography of IS Spokesman Abu Muhammad al-Adnani as-Shami', 1 November 2014, at: https://pietervanostaeyen.wordpress.com

6. 'ISIS Declares Establishment of Islamic Caliphate, Appoints ISIS Leader Abu Bakr Al-Baghdadi as "Caliph"', *MEMRI: Jihad and Terrorism Threat Monitor*, 29 June 2014, at: www.memrijttm.org

7. Ibid.

8. Ibid.

9. Hannah Strange, 'Islamic State Leader Abu Bakr al-Baghdadi addresses Muslims in Mosul', *Daily Telegraph*, 5 July 2014.

10. Abu Bakr al-Baghdadi's Message as Caliph, 'A Message to the Mujahidin and the Muslim Ummah in the Month of Ramadan', Gatestone Institute, 2 July 2013, at: www.gatestoneinstitute.org/documents/baghdadi-caliph. pdf

11. Christoph Reuter, 'Video Games and Cigarettes: Syria's Disneyland for Jihadists', *Spiegel*, 27 September 2013; Robin Yassin-Kassab, '"There's No Hope Left": The Syrian Refugee Camp that is Becoming a Township', *Guardian*, 18 February 2014.

12. 'British Jihadi Compares Syria War to Call of Duty', *BBC News*, 13 June 2014; Thomas Hegghammer, 'Syria's Foreign Fighters', *Foreign Policy*, 9 December 2013.

13. Ibid.

14. Reuter, 'Video Games and Cigarettes'.

15. 'It Ain't Half Hot Here, Mum', *The Economist*, 30 August 2014.

16. 'Jihadists Cut Down 150-year-old Oak in Syria', *Naharnet*, 22 December 2013.

17. Abu Bakr al-Baghdadi's Message as Caliph.

18. Tom Perry, 'Islamic State Recruits at Record Pace in Syria: Monitor', *Reuters*, 19 August 2014; Greg Miller, 'Airstrikes Against Islamic State Do Not Seem to Have Affected Flow of Fighters to Syria', *Washington Post*, 30 October 2014.

19. Yaroslav Trofimov, 'In Islamic State Stronghold of Raqqa, Foreign Fighters Dominate', *Wall Street Journal*, 5 February 2015; Lina Khatib, 'The Human Dimension of Life Under the Islamic State', Carnegie Middle East Center, 4 March 2015.

20. 'It Ain't Half Hot Here, Mum'; Daveed Gartenstein-Ross, 'How Many Fighters Does the Islamic State Really Have?' *War on the Rocks*, 9 February 2015, at: http://warontherocks.com

21. Peter R. Neumann, 'Foreign Fighter Total in Syria/Iraq Now Exceeds 20,000; Surpasses Afghanistan Conflict in the 1980s', International Centre for the Study of Radicalisation and Political Violence, 26 January

2015; Trofimov, 'In Islamic State Stronghold of Raqqa, Foreign Fighters Dominate'.

22. Gartenstein-Ross, 'How Many Fighters Does the Islamic State Really Have?'

17. Inside the Whale

1. Michael D. Shear and Eric Schmitt, 'In Raid to Save Foley and Other Hostages, U.S. Found None', *New York Times*, 20 August 2014; Nicholas Schmidle, 'Inside the Failed Raid to Save Foley and Sotloff', *New Yorker*, 5 September 2014; John Cantlie, 'Hard Talk: The Real Story Behind My Videos', *Dabiq*, No. 4, at: http://tinyurl.com/mtddsb6

2. Paul Lewis, Spencer Ackerman and Saeed Kamali Dehghan, 'Iraq Crisis: Barack Obama Sends in US Troops as Isis Insurgency Worsens', *Guardian*, 17 June 2014; Jacob Siegel, 'Even Former Commandos Call Iraq "an Impossible Mission"', *Daily Beast*, 24 June 2014; Rebecca Kaplan, 'How Many U.S. Troops Are Currently in Iraq?' CBS News, 1 July 2014; Spencer Ackerman and Tom McCarthy, 'Barack Obama Doubles US Troop Levels for War Against Isis in Iraq', *Guardian*, 8 November 2014.

3. Liz Sly, 'U.S.-backed Syria Rebels Routed by Fighters Linked to Al-Qaeda', *Washington Post*, 2 November 2014; 'President Obama Needs to Fix his Flawed Islamic State Policy', *Washington Post*, 18 November 2014.

4. Scott Creighton, 'ISIS Drives Texas-made Toyota Trucks Apparently Modified for U.S. Special Forces', 10 September 2014, https://willyloman.wordpress.com

5. '"Hundreds Killed" in Syrian Gas Field Capture', *Al Jazeera*, 19 July 2014.

6. Jennifer Cafarella, 'ISIS Works to Merge its Northern Front across Iraq and Syria', Institute for the Study of War, 9 August 2014; Kristen Gillespie and Joseph Adams, 'Prelude to a Massacre: The Downfall of A-Raqqa', Syria Direct, 2 December 2014.

7. 'Infographic: Anatomy of an IS Massacre Part I', Syria Direct, 3 December 2014; 'Infographic: Anatomy of an IS Massacre Part II', Syria Direct, 7 December 2014.

8. 'The Punishing of Shu'aytat for Treachery', *Dabiq*, No. 3, at: http://tinyurl.com/nj3xuvn; Liz Sly, 'Syria Tribal Revolt Against Islamic State Ignored, Fueling Resentment', *Washington Post*, 20 October 2014; 'Shaitat Return to Deir e-Zor After Pledging Fealty to IS', Syria Direct, 27 November 2014.

9. Sly, 'Syria Tribal Revolt Against Islamic State Ignored, Fuelling Resentment'.

10. Loveday Morris, 'Razing of Mosul's Shrines Sparks First Signs of Resistance Against Islamic State', *Washington Post*, 30 July 2014; 'ISIS Militants Blow Up Jonah's Tomb', *Guardian*, 24 July 2014; Jean Marc Mojon and Ammar Karimi, 'In Mosul, Resistance Against ISIS Rises from the City's Rubble', *Daily Star*, 31 July 2014.

11. Aymenn Jawad Al-Tamimi, 'Sunni Opposition to the Islamic State', *Middle East Review of International Affairs*, Vol. 18, No. 3 (Fall 2014).

12. Steve Hopkins, 'Full Horror of the Yazidis Who Didn't Escape Mount Sinjar, *Daily Mail,* 14 October 2014.

13. 'Report of the Office of the UN High Commissioner for Human Rights on the Human Rights Situation in Iraq in the Light of Abuses Committed by the So-Called Islamic State in Iraq and the Levant and Associated Groups', UN High Commission for Human Rights, 13 March 2015; Letta Taylor, 'The Silence Over the Islamic State's Abuse of Women', Human Rights Watch, 25 November 2014.

14. Tracey Shelton, '"If it Wasn't for the Kurdish Fighters, We Would Have Died Up There"', *Global Post*, 27 August 2014; Martin Chulov, Julian Borger, Richard Norton-Taylor, Dan Roberts, 'US Troops Land on Mt Sinjar to Plan for Yazidi Evacuation', *Guardian*, 13 August 2014.

15. Cantlie, 'Hard Talk: The Real Story Behind My Videos'.

18.   *Euphrates Volcano*

1. Fehim Taştekin, 'Turkish Tomb in Syria Becomes Flashpoint for Conflict', *Al-Monitor*, 27 March 2014.

2. Taştekin, 'Turkish Tomb in Syria'; Mahdi Darius Nazemroaya, 'Suleiman Shah and Turkey's Election Invasion of Syria: Wag the Dog Turkish-Style', Strategic Culture Foundation, 30 March 2014.

3. Nick Tattersall, 'Turkey Calls Syria Security Leak "Villainous", Blocks YouTube', *Reuters*, 27 March 2014; 'YouTube Ban: How Turkish Officials Conspired to Stage Syria Attack to Provoke War', *RT*, 28 March 2014, at: http://rt.com/news/turkey-syria-phone-leak-861/

4. Karen Leigh, 'Q+A: On Foreign Fighters Flowing Into Syria', *Syria Deeply*, 2 December 2013, at: www.syriadeeply.org/articles/2013/12/2628/qa-foreign-fighters-flowing-syria/

5. Gareth Jenkins, 'Lies and Videotape: Trucks, Weapons and Turkey's Spiraling Descent', *The Turkey Analyst*, 3 June 2015; Fehim Taştekin,

'Turkish Military Says MIT Shipped Weapons to al-Qaeda', *Al-Monitor*, 15 January 2015.

6. David L. Phillips, 'Research Paper: ISIS-Turkey Links', Institute for the Study of Human Rights, 9 November 2014; Daniel Pipes, 'More on Turkish Support for ISIS', 18 June 2014, at: www.danielpipes.org / blog/2014/06/more-on-turkish-support-for-isis

7. 'The ISIS-Ankara Oil Pipeline', The Rojava Report, 15 September 2014, at: https://rojavareport.wordpress.com/2014/09/15/the-isis-ankara-oil-pipeline/

8. David E. Sanger and Julie Hirschfeld Davis, 'Struggling to Starve ISIS of Oil Revenue, U.S. Seeks Assistance From Turkey', *New York Times*, 13 September 2014; Thomas Seibert, 'Is NATO Ally Turkey Tacitly Fueling the ISIS War Machine? *Daily Beast*, 8 September 2014; 'The ISIS-Ankara Oil Pipeline'.

9. John Caves, 'Syrian Kurds and the Democratic Union Party (PYD)', Institute for the Study of War, 6 December 2012; Carl Drott, 'The Syrian Experiment with "Apoism"', Carnegie Endowment for International Peace, 20 May 2014.

10. Piotr Zalewski, 'Syria's Many Battlefields: Islamist Rebels Wage War Against the Kurds', *Time*, 26 September 2013; Carl Drott, 'Arab Tribes Split Between Kurds and Jihadists', Carnegie Endowment for International Peace, 15 May 2014; Patrick Cockburn, 'Isis in Syria: The Kurdish Enclave Still Resisting the Tyranny of President Assad and the Militant Fighters', *Independent*, 27 May 2015.

11. Zalewski, 'Syria's Many Battlefields: Islamist Rebels Wage War Against the Kurds'.

12. Semih Idiz, 'Why is Jabhat al-Nusra No Longer Useful to Turkey?' *US News and World Report*, 11 June 2014.

13. Amberin Zaman, 'Islamic State Uses Turkish Consulate in Mosul as Headquarters', *Al-Monitor*, 17 July 2014; Tulin Daloglu, 'ISIS Raises Flag at Turkish Border', *Al-Monitor*, 30 June 2014.

14. Bill Gertz, 'ISIS Moving Hundreds of Captured Iraqi Tanks and Armoured Vehicles to Syria', *Washington Free Beacon*, 17 June 2014, at: http://tinyurl.com/oppww6h; Zaman, 'Islamic State Uses Turkish Consulate in Mosul as Headquarters'.

15. Katherine Wilkens, 'A Kurdish Alamo: Five Reasons the Battle for Kobane Matters', Carnegie Endowment for International Peace, 10 October 2014; Aron Lund, 'Why the Victory in Kobane Matters', Carnegie Endowment for International Peace, 13 February 2015.

16. Thomas Seibert, 'The Turks to ISIS: "Let's Make a Deal"', *Daily Beast*, 21 September 2014; Johnlee Varghese, 'Turkey Swapped 180 ISIS Fighters Including 2 British Jihadists for its Mosul Embassy Staff', *International Business Times*, 6 October 2014.

17. Lyse Doucet, 'Islamic State Crisis: Turkish PM Rejects Kobane Criticism', BBC News, 28 October 2014.

18. Phillips, 'Research Paper: ISIS-Turkey Links'.

19. Leo Benedictus, 'Why Did Turkey Invade Syria to Dig Up the Grave of Suleyman Shah?' *Guardian*, 23 February 2015; David A. Graham, 'The Surreal Saga of Suleyman Shah', *The Atlantic*, 24 February 2015.

Postscript: Saddam's Ghost

1. Robert Spencer, 'Islamic State: "We Will Conquer Your Rome, Break Your Crosses, and Enslave Your Women, By the Permission of Allah"', *Jihad Watch*, 21 September 2014.

2. 'Counter-ISIL Military Coalition Concludes Operational Planning Conference', United States Central Command, 1 May 2015.

3. Lizzie Dearden, 'Syria Air Strikes: US Targeted Khorasan Terrorist Group to Stop "Imminent Attack"', *Independent*, 23 September 2014.

4. Ibid; 'By The Numbers', *Washington Wire*, 17 October 2014; Richard Norton-Taylor, 'Scale of UK Attacks on Islamic State in Iraq', *The Guardian*, 11 May 2015.

5. Kerry Sheridan, 'Iraq Death Toll Reaches 500,000 Since Start Of U.S.-Led Invasion, New Study Says', *Agence France-Presse*, 23 January 2014; 'Iraqi Deaths From Violence 2003–2011', Iraq Body Count, at: www.iraqbodycount.org/analysis/numbers/2011/; 'Syrian Civil War Death Toll Rises to More Than 191,300, According to UN', *Guardian*, 22 August 2014; Samuel Smith, 'UN Report on ISIS: 24,000 Killed, Injured by Islamic State; Children Used as Soldiers, Women Sold as Sex Slaves', *Christian Post*, 9 October 2014.

6. 'Kerry: Saving Kobane not part of strategy', *Al Jazeera*, 13 October 2014.

7. Spencer Ackerman, 'Pentagon Denies US Strategy to Defeat ISIS Jihadists is Unravelling', *Guardian*, 5 November 2014.

8. 'By The Numbers'.

9. Eric Schmitt, 'Obstacles Limit Targets and Pace of Strikes in ISIS', *New York Times*, 9 November 2014.

10. Eric Schmitt, 'US Adds Planes to Bolster Drive to Wipe Out ISIS', *New York Times*, 26 November 2014.
11. 'Kerry: Saving Kobane Not Part of Strategy'.
12. Robin Wright, 'Imagining a Remapped Middle East', *New York Times*, 28 September 2013; Ralph Peters, 'Blood Borders: How a Better Middle East Would Look', *Armed Forces Journal*, 1 June 2006.

Index